ISBN 978-1-333-08372-4
PIBN 10455129

This book is a reproduction of an important historical work. Forgotten Books uses state-of-the-art technology to digitally reconstruct the work, preserving the original format whilst repairing imperfections present in the aged copy. In rare cases, an imperfection in the original, such as a blemish or missing page, may be replicated in our edition. We do, however, repair the vast majority of imperfections successfully; any imperfections that remain are intentionally left to preserve the state of such historical works.

1 MONTH OF
FREE
READING

at
www.ForgottenBooks.com

By purchasing this book you are eligible for one month membership to ForgottenBooks.com, giving you unlimited access to our entire collection of over 700,000 titles via our web site and mobile apps.

To claim your free month visit:
www.forgottenbooks.com/free455129

English
Français
Deutsche
Italiano
Español
Português

www.forgottenbooks.com

Mythology Photography **Fiction**
Fishing Christianity **Art** Cooking
Essays Buddhism Freemasonry
Medicine **Biology** Music **Ancient
Egypt** Evolution Carpentry Physics
Dance Geology **Mathematics** Fitness
Shakespeare **Folklore** Yoga Marketing
Confidence Immortality Biographies
Poetry **Psychology** Witchcraft
Electronics Chemistry History **Law**
Accounting **Philosophy** Anthropology
Alchemy Drama Quantum Mechanics
Atheism Sexual Health **Ancient History**
Entrepreneurship Languages Sport
Paleontology Needlework Islam
Metaphysics Investment Archaeology
Parenting Statistics Criminology
Motivational

Anglo-Russian Literary
Society
Proceedings
no.71 (1914)

THE

ANGLO-RUSSIAN

LITERARY SOCIETY

(FOUNDED IN 1893)

(THE IMPERIAL INSTITUTE, LONDON, S.W.)

PROCEEDINGS

OCTOBER, NOVEMBER AND DECEMBER, 1914

taining Report of Proceedings on Post-Bellum Peace Movement
9 Dec 1914

PRINTED FOR THE SOCIETY

MDCCCCXIV.

ENTERED AT STATIONERS' HALL

THE

ANGLO-RUSSIAN
LITERARY SOCIETY

(FOUNDED IN 1893)

(THE IMPERIAL INSTITUTE, LONDON, S.W.)

PROCEEDINGS

October, November and December, 1914.

PRINTED FOR THE SOCIETY

MDCCCCXIV.

ENTERED AT STATIONERS' HALL

LONDON:

THE ARMY AND NAVY CO-OPERATIVE SOCIETY, LIMITED,

105, VICTORIA STREET, WESTMINSTER, S.W.

THE ANGLO-RUSSIAN LITERARY SOCIETY

THE ANGLO-RUSSIAN LITERARY SOCIETY

THE IMPERIAL INSTITUTE

IMPERIAL INSTITUTE ROAD, LONDON, S.W.

OBJECTS OF THE SOCIETY.

1.—To promote the study of the Russian Language and Literature.

2.—To form a Library of Russian books and other works, especially interesting from an Anglo-Russian point of view.

3.—To take in Russian Periodicals and Newspapers.

4.—To hold monthly meetings periodically, for the reading and discussion of suitable papers, writing and speaking in English or Russian being alike admissible.

5.—To promote friendly relations between Great Britain and Russia.

A 2

2

CONTENTS.

CONTENTS.

RULES

1.—That the management of the Society be vested in a Committee consisting of a President, Honorary Secretary and Treasurer, and five other members, and that of this Committee three shall form a quorum.

2.—That vacancies on the Committee be filled up by the unanimous vote of the Committee.

3.—That applications for membership be made to the Committee. Members will be admitted by the unanimous consent of the Committee.

4.—That members residing in or within fifteen miles of London shall pay an annual subscription of one guinea, and that those residing beyond that distance, or abroad, shall pay an annual subscription of half-a-guinea. Members residing in Russia may pay five roubles.

5.—That all subscriptions be payable in advance.

6 —That ladies may become members and take part in the debates.

7.—That honorary members and correspondents may be elected by the unanimous consent of the Committee.

8.—That visitors may be introduced, and take part in the proceedings on the proposition of two members, and with the sanction of the Committee. Visitors' names will be entered in a special book.

9.—That Annual Meetings shall be summoned and provision made for special meetings, if necessary.

10.—That members or others wishing to open debates, read papers, or give lectures before the Society, be requested to give notice to the Committee, allowing time to prepare the programme for each quarter in advance.

11.—That any questions of procedure not determined by these rules shall be dealt with by the Committee.

October 7th, 1914.

The President, Mr. E. A. Cazalet, in the Chair.

I.

THE EUROPEAN UNITY LEAGUE IN THE PAST BEFORE THE WAR.

By Major C. Freeman Murray.

Sir Max Waechter, the founder of the European Unity League, has for many years devoted his chief attention to the difficult, almost insuperable problem of how such a fearful calamity as the present general European War could be avoided. He came to the conclusion that the only way in which such a war could possibly be avoided was by bringing the two opposed camps of the Triple Alliance and Triple Entente together in amity, not as enemies but as allies, on the basis of the fundamental unity of their deepest economic interests; that is to say, the fundamental unity of their financial, commercial, and labour interests, all of which were threatened with something like ruin by the occurrence of such a war.

In pursuance of this idea he visited all the sovereigns of Europe and interviewed the principal statesmen of the countries concerned, and, to put the matter shortly, was everywhere informed that they would help in every way to bring about so desirable a consummation, IF and when public opinion in the various nations could be that way inclined. With such assurances from all the highest quarters, the matter manifestly resolved itself into a question of the education of public opinion in the direction of

European unity. At first sight this might seem a hopeless task; but recollect that the sovereigns of Europe were favourable to the idea, and that the financial, the commercial classes, and the labour classes could also be depended upon if their opinion could only be organised. It was, at least, well worth trying.

So Sir Max Waechter founded the European Unity League, its official object being described as: "To bring about a good understanding amongst the Great Powers of Europe."

The League began active operations in April, 1914. It started then with the idea of firmly establishing itself during 1914 in Great Britain, and then in 1915 establishing branches in every country of Europe. The League started to form a strong Advisory Committee for the British Branch, in which it made wonderful progress, and in four months' work had obtained a Committee of 400 members of all classes, every one of whom was a proved man of affairs, with not a single unknown or unrepresentative man amongst them. The Council included, for example, no less than 100 well-known admirals and generals. This would have been gradually extended so as to embrace 400 prominent peers, M.P.'s and public servants, 400 prominent capitalists, and 400 prominent Labour leaders by the end of 1914. Every day saw the adhesion of new members of importance. Then suddenly, like a bolt from the blue, came the sudden outburst of the present catastrophic European War, shattering at one blow the fair hope of the League. But it is only for a time. Behind the clouds of War the sun of Peace is still shining, and when those clouds eventually roll away from a sorely stricken Europe, the League will resume its efforts, this time with, not the hope, but the certainty of final success.

II.
THE EUROPEAN UNITY LEAGUE DURING THE PRESENT WAR TIME.

THE difference in the work of the League before the war and after the war will be very great. Before the war it had to address itself to a public strangely apathetic and disposed to dub as " alarmists " those who stated unpleasant truths or prophesied events unpleasant to think of. This was a great and very real obstacle to progress. It will exist no more. After the war the League will address itself to a public every individual of whom will have been converted to the views of the League by the terrible logic of events. In this connection I will quote a short extract from an admirable article in the September number of *The Round Table* called " Lombard Street in War " :—

There is no banker, no merchant, no trader, no shopkeeper in the civilised world whose business has not been affected. There are few civilised countries in which a moratorium, or something equivalent to it, is not now in force. In the Continental countries of Europe actually at war, industry is to a large extent at a standstill. The result on these great industrial nations cannot but be tremendous. Their foreign trade alone (in peace) totals about £2,400,000,000.

If we estimate roughly that 14,000,000 men are under arms, and that one man can produce £100 of wealth in a year, we have at once a direct loss of £1,400,000,000, apart altogether from any indirect loss due to the dislocation of trade and finance and the enormous number of men thrown out of work indirectly by the war.

Let no country (neutral or otherwise) suppose that it is going to escape the consequences of this great cataclysm. The purchasing power of the *world* will have been very seriously diminished, and it cannot be long before the enormous loss of capital will make itself felt. There is then likely to be a prolonged period of very great depression.

I need say nothing more about the war, except that when it is over all men will say, " Never again ! " and will unite to translate that universal dictum into concerted action.

The League is of course at present, during the war, in a state of waiting. It must remain so until peace is in sight. But it adheres to the object and to the programme with which it started. These are set forth in the two documents which I will now read to you :--

(1) The *Post-bellum* Object of the League,
(2) The Programme of the League,

printed forms of which are herewith attached.

THE *POST-BELLUM* OBJECT OF THE LEAGUE.

To PROMOTE A FRIENDLY UNDERSTANDING BETWEEN THE SIX GREAT POWERS OF EUROPE.

Extract from the Dispatch of the Minister for Foreign Affairs to the British Embassy in Berlin.

No. 101.

Sir EDWARD GREY to Sir E. GOSCHEN,
FOREIGN OFFICE, July 30th, 1914.

And I will say this: If the Peace of Europe can be preserved, and the present crisis safely passed, my own endeavour will be to promote some arrangement to which Germany could be a party, by which she could be assured that no aggressive or hostile policy would be pursued against her or her allies by France, Russia, and ourselves, jointly or separately. I have desired this and worked for it, as far as I could, through the last Balkan crisis, and, Germany having a corresponding object, our relations sensibly improved. This idea has hitherto been too Utopian to form the subject of definite proposals, but if this present crisis, so much more acute than any that Europe has gone through for generations, be safely passed, I am hopeful that the RELIEF AND REACTION WHICH WILL FOLLOW MAY MAKE POSSIBLE SOME MORE DEFINITE *RAPPROCHEMENT* BETWEEN THE POWERS THAN HAS BEEN POSSIBLE HITHERTO.

It is desired to call your attention to the fact that the "hope" herein expressed by the Minister for Foreign Affairs exactly coincides with the "Object" of the European Unity League. The bitterness of feeling which will follow the war will be very great, and the consequent possibility of further war of revenge is one against which every possible organized effort should be directed. Ou the other hand, the reaction after the war in favour of some permanent international guarantee against a repetition of such stupendous calamities will afford a most fruitful ground for the successful propaganda of our Object, provided that we are ready and strong enough to properly utilise it. We now know officially that the "hope" of our Foreign Offiee is identical with the *post-bellum* Object of our League, and we intend to do our utmost, directly the war is over, to prepare public opinion in every country of Europe for the realisation of the *rapprochement* hoped for by Sir Edward Grey. We therefore think it desirable to continue the activity of the League -during the war so far as is possible. We shall endeavour during the war to build up the League on the firmest foundation and to the greatest strength possible, in order that directly the war is over we may be in a position to take effective action to prepare public opinion in every country towards the desired end.

Towards this aim your consideration and assistance is earnestly requested.

ORGANIZING SECRETARY.

The desire of the League is to perhaps resume modified operations in the direction of strengthening still further the Advisory Council on the representative lines previously explained, as soon as circumstances permit and the time becomes propitious. When that psychological moment will arrive it is at present impossible to say. At present it is not possible for men in Great Britain to think of anything, or do anything, other than that which will conduce to the success of our arms. This will continue to be the case as long as there is any danger to be apprehended from the enemy. It will continue until the enemy has been forced to abandon all hope of victory, and is obviously merely continuing the contest with their last resources in order to obtain better terms of peace. When that period arrives, when peace appears in sight once more, the League proposes to resume its operations. Its object in doing so will be that it may become sufficiently strong before the actual end of the war to be able to take effective international action *directly* peace is declared. That is our desire and our hope. In the meantime we must wait.

III.

THE LEAGUE IN THE FUTURE, AFTER THE WAR.

After the war the League will endeavour to carry out as quickly and completely as possible the programme which I have already read out to you.

I will not here embark on any foolish prophecies of what the *post-bellum* settlement of Europe will be, for at present any such attempt would be the merest guess-work. Of one thing only we can be sure, and that is that it will be of such a nature as to preclude a repetition of the present war of desolation and ruin. If the peace of Europe cannot by politics alone be assured for ever, at least it will be assured for many years to come as far as the utmost efforts of diplomatists and statesmen can go.

In addition to, and beyond and above and below the
actual political *post-bellum* re-settlement of European
nations and boundaries and power, there will be an
enormous concensus of public opinion that a general
European war must NEVER occur again, as too ruinous
to the most fundamental economic interests and to the
economic life of Europe. To this great concensus of
public opinion the European Unity League will address
itself, and strive to produce concerted action on the various
nations of Europe on the lines laid down in our programme
which is before you.

In this programme you will observe that the League
does not include political action or propaganda or discussion, as too argumentative, heating and disruptive. The
League proposes to confine its action to emphasising and
intensifying the sense of the economic unity of Europe,
the unity of the most fundamental financial, commercial and
labour interests throughout all the nations of the European
family. It is hoped that the League will thus be able to
do most valuable work and, by preparing public opinion,
prepare the ground for further political action eventually in
the direction of political unity.

After the war there will remain a terrible legacy of
national and racial bitterness, which it should be the business of all friends of European unity to minimise and
smooth away as far as possible. This will be one of the
chief objects of the European Unity League, though, as it
has not yet been put before our Council, it is not at present
possible to say what curative measures the League will
attempt.

At this moment, whilst the critical period of the war is
still in progress, there is little more that can at present be
said about the European Unity League. At present we
can think of the war and the war only. When peace is

once more in sight, when the right psychological moment arrives, the League will resume its efforts on the lines which I have endeavoured to lay before you, and which are outlined in our printed programme. Meantime we must wait until the storm of death and ruin and desolation which is passing over Europe shall have passed away.

As this paper is being read before the Anglo-Russian Society, I should like to make one suggestion for discussion on my own account, not on account of the League. It is this. That one of the best means of minimising the racial bitterness which will be left behind by the war will be the better education of the public in the elements of European anthropology. Racial enthusiasts require to be taught that there are no such things as pure races. People require to be taught that all the nations of Europe are merely diverse "blends" in varying proportions of the same three original strains—Mediterranean, Nordic or Teutonic, Alpine or Celto-Slavonic. For instance, one hears so much of the struggle between Slav and Teuton. But the typical German is really a mixture of Teuton and Slav, of Teutonic-Slavonic blood, the Slav characteristic elements, if anything, predominating in the majority (*vide* Deniker, " The Races of Man "). So that all the talk of Slav and German being of naturally hostile races is false anthropology and false history. This, no doubt, sounds to you a truism. So it is, partly, but not wholly. To many people it is not a truism. I think that much valuable work might be done, from a political standpoint, by educating the people to understand the racial unity of Europe. And the chief factor in this racial unity lies in the intermixture of Celto-Slavonic blood common to us all —Russians, Germans, French, Italians, British. The more this fact can be substantiated and popularised, the less we shall hear of racial antagonism, and the more we shall hear of the racial unity of Europe, which again will be a help to the economic unity of Europe, and the two together to the political unity of Europe.

THE DISCUSSION.

The PRESIDENT spoke in high terms of Sir Max Waechter's noble ideals of peace consolidation, and recalled his own old schoolmaster's words uttered more than half-a-century ago :—

When one man kills another he is a murderer, and when many men kill many others they are all heroes.

Mr. CAZALET spoke also of the Hague Peace Conference, in which great and good men had taken part. Among them were: M. Leon Bourgeois, the representative of France, and Mr. Andrew Dickson White, who told us in his "Autobiography" that the German Emperor appeared to favour arbitration, but Count Münster was against it. The speaker drew attention to the "Peace Year Book of 1914," which contained the names of hundreds of peace societies all over the world. These numerous societies should all join hands under the leadership of the European Unity League, uniting their forces to attain the same good end, for blessed are the peace-makers. In thanking Major Murray for his excellent lecture, the President said it was an ingenious idea, which suggested that all nations—even Slavs and Germans—came of the same stock, and should, therefore, be brothers and friends!

There is, however, an old Russian saying, attributed to the time of Ivan the Terrible :—

A German, be he even a good man, it is always better to hang him.

It may be added that in vulgar Russian every foreigner was called a German (*Niemetz, i.e.* the dumb man).

Mme. DE PERROT regretted the constant abuse of our German enemies, and recommended more moderation and less expression of passionate resentment during the sad and trying period through which we were now passing.

Mr. W. ENSOM explained that he attended as a visitor, being a member of the European Unity League. He said he and his wife (who was present) were old residents of New Zealand, and had been long interested in all movements that had for their object the abolition of war and the substitution of arbitration for the present methods.

Referring to the paper which had just been read, the general tenor of which he endorsed, he said he agreed with the gentleman who had opened the debate, that the Unity League should not remain inactive during the present crisis, but on the contrary, now that the public mind was so much agitated on the question of international relations, it was time to press forward the advocacy of a policy of conciliation and international good will.

What was needed was a strong effort to counteract a tendency observable in the Press of this country to magnify and give prominence to those matters and incidents likely to stir up hatred and bitterness, and in some cases circulating false news as to the conduct of the enemy. All wars were awful, and incidents occurred in the heat of conflict that were inexcusable. What was needed was a spirit of fairness and forbearance towards those we were opposing, which could only lay a secure foundation for some permanent and fair settlement, and also help forward the idea of the Unity League.

Dr. COUNSEL, having dealt with the lecture, expressed the hope that by the time this war was over Sir Max Waechter's League might well become a World Unity League of all the civilized nations, in the interest of civilization and freedom and against war under modern conditions.

That at long last the Russian and English Empires are standing together, with France and glorious little Belgium, one in this desperate struggle, in a war such as the world has never yet seen, in defence of small nationalities, of free democratic government and of civilization, must be a source of great satisfaction to Mr. Cazalet and those who have been working with him in this Anglo-Russian Society for the promotion of better relations between the nations.

And surely it promises well for the future of Russia and the peoples within her Empire that her first-declared object in this war is to free the Polish provinces from the yoke of Prussia and Austria, and give Poland once more a place amongst the free nations of the world.

Rev. R. S. LATIMER, in moving a cordial vote of thanks to the author and the reader of the paper, reminded the meeting of the great and constant service rendered for many years to the cause of international peace by the witness of the Society of Friends. He believed that the present European War, calling forth as it did the warmest of friendships between the allied nations and evoking the heartiest expressions of goodwill, was laying sure foundations for enduring peace hereafter. Such societies as theirs, too, cultivating as they did an appreciation of the literature of the mutual nations, played no inconsiderable part in the same direction.

In seconding the vote of thanks Dr. POLLEN said he thought it was hardly necessary to say anything to commend it to the meeting. They were all very grateful to

Major Murray, and appreciated the objects of the " Unity "
he advocated.

As to what the lady speaker had said of the constant
abuse of our German enemies, Dr. Pollen reminded his
audience that the great Duke of Wellington never lost an
English gun and never spoke against a *foe.* He had, however, some very nasty things to say of his allies, the
Germans, and their thieving and slaughtering propen-
sities, and their desire to sack Paris after the Battle of
Waterloo.

As to war : no one deplored it more than he (Dr. Pollen)
did, but it was hard to say whether war was a cause or a
consequence. He looked upon all nationalities—Slav,
Teuton, Celt—as friends and brother souls, and he wished
that wars might cease. But the first step to ensuring that
was to control human passions, and put down pride, ambition, jealousy, and fear. And the next best step was to
get the peoples to understand the peoples, and this could be
best achieved by the spread of an international language;
and being connected with an association for the spread of
such a language* he was in close accord with the society
which Major Murray represented. With regard to what
the lecturer had said about Russia, Dr. Pollen read the
following lines, written by him in 1891, which he said had
in them somewhat of prophetic strain :—

ENGLAND, RUSSIA AND INDIA.

Russia, farewell ! ere leaving thee
 I learned to love thy much-wronged race,
Thy mis-read past aright to see,
 Thy glorious destiny to trace,
To know thee as thon truly art
 (Whate'er thy slanderous foes may bawl),
A people great, with kindly heart,
 Helping the hurt, forgiving all.

* Esperanto.

Alone against Napoleon's pride,
  When Europe groaned beneath his sway,
Did'st thou arise and roll the tide
  Of conquest back, and hold thy way
Till thy victorious banners flew
  Across the sunny vines of France,
And well the streets of Paris knew
  Thy Cossacks' and thy Uhlans' lance.
Thou for the faith of Christendom
  Stood'st ever firm against the Turk,
And many a rescued Christian home
  Doth bless to-day thy holy work.
When jealous Europe 'gainst thee strove,
  How nobly did'st thou stand at bay !
And Sebastópol's heights can prove
  How brave thou wast in trial's day !
And all that woe against thee wrought
  Thou hast in full forgiven, forgot ;
The foes who then against thee fought
  As foes are now regarded not.

Then, England, pause, know friend from foe !
  Where, when, has Russia crossed thy path ?
That she doth ever greater grow
  This seems the greatest fault she hath.
In truth, the " Teuton " is thy foe !
  Thy rival he, in every field ;
His power thy Court—thy councils—know,
  Thy commerce naught from him can shield ;
His princes lead thy daughters forth
  Dowered deep in dowers of English gold ;
His merchant vessels sweep thy north ;
  Thy "silver streak " his warships hold.
He threatens thee on every side ;
  While thou dost bend to him and yield,
Surrendering to his growing pride
  The best of thy colonial field.
He stirs the Russ against thy power—
  Pointing to plains of Hindustan—
Hoping to stay the dreaded hour
  When France will meet him, man to man.

But why should England cross the Russ ?
  Our friend of old—our Ally true !

Asia is wide ; for him, for us,
There's space to spare and work to do.
Redeem the cradle of our race—
Let commerce circle everywhere—
Let love regain its pride of place—
Let Eden once more blossom there!
Let " great white Czar," let " great white Queen "
Stretch forth o'er Asia healing hands,
Touching the sere leaf into green,
Blessing with bloom the barren lands!

England and Russia—friendly Powers!
India secure, and strong and free--
Over the West no war-cloud lowers—
The East regains its liberty.

J, POLLEN.

St. Leonards, 1891.

NOVEMBER 3RD, 1914.

DR. POLLEN, C.I.E., IN THE CHAIR.

NOTES ON
PERSIA—PAST AND PRESENT.

By E. A. CAZALET.

AN old authority tells us that the early history of Persia is lost in remote antiquity, and for authentic accounts the uncertain gleanings of oral tradition, or the fictions of poets, have been substituted. Anyhow, it is a sad and sanguinary story. The Shahnameh of Firdousi, the Homer of Persia, is a legendary history of the kings. From this and similar authorities, Sir John Malcolm compiled the early annals of Persia.

Cyrus the Elder, whose name as a world conqueror is popularly linked with those of Alexander the Great, of Cæsar, of Gengis Khan and Napoleon, conquered Babylon, and on its ruins founded Persia. Greek historians call him the hardy chief of a pastoral horde, who vanquished his wealthy and luxurious neighbours.

It is needless to weary you with legendary descriptions of the fabulous high deeds of Cyrus the Younger, of Darius, who was conquered by Alexander the Great, Xerxes and the Artaxerxes. The old story is unfortunately ever new :—

Those take who can, and those keep who have the power.

The Romans, and, later, the Arabian tribes, under the standard of Mahomet, subverted in one common ruin the manners and most sacred institutions of the country.

In A.D. 1072 Mulik Shah's dominion extended from the Mediterranean to the Wall of China. From the decline of his dynasty to the conquest by the son of the mighty

Genghis Khan, Persia was distracted by the contests of rival chiefs, known as the Atábaks.

In the seventeenth century Persia flourished under the great Shah Abbas. His successors were vanquished by Mahmud Ghilzy, who entered Persia at the head of 25,000 Afghans and became the king of the country in 1722. But Russian and Turkish armies invaded Persia, and the inhabitants of Kazvin rose in insurrection and expelled the Afghan garrison from the place. Mahmud was seriously alarmed, and conceived the horrible design of exterminating the conquered people of Persia. Nadir-Kuli, a well-known Persian chief, finally expelled the Afghans, who had devastated Persia for seven years.

Nadir Shah, as he was now called, defeated the Turks, subdued Afghanistan, and his triumphant legions entered India and reached Delhi, which made no resistance. But the glory of foreign conquest was tarnished by domestic tyranny. Nadir was wounded by an assassin, who fired on him from a wood. His suspicion fell on his own son Riza, whom he caused to be deprived of eyesight.

The death of Nadir involved the country in the greatest distraction. Karim Khan, a sagacious and courageous chief, finally became the ruler. The generous confidence with which he treated those whom he forgave never failed to attach them to his person.

Aghá Muhammad Khan was a strong but intensely cruel Shah. His nephew, Fath Ali Shah, drifted into war with Russia, which was to his detriment. Later on, encouraged by Russia, he marched on Herat, contrary to British interests ; he also allowed Russia to have complete supremacy in the Caspian Sea. After various intrigues and complicated negotiations the Persians finished by seizing Herat. England then declared war on Persia, and General Outram, whom the Indian Government placed in supreme command, sailed from

Bombay, on the 16th of January, 1857, for the Persian Gulf. The superior numbers of the Persians were totally defeated. So severe was the lesson that even the disasters of the Indian revolt could not induce the Shah to venture once more on a rupture with England.

I may now refer to my late dear old friend the Baron de Bode, whose " Travels in Luristan and Arabistan " appeared in London during the middle of the last century.* When residing in Persia he was much appreciated by the King of the day, Muhammed Shah, who said he valued Baron de Bode because he always spoke the truth, an exceptional virtue in the East, and even in the North, South and West.

The Baron, whose hobby was travel, decided to explore the route of Alexander the Great, which extends along the northern shore of the Persian Gulf. He considered himself fortunate in having obtained letters from the Shah to pass through the territory of the great Bakhtiyari chief, whose unruly subjects were freebooters.

But what was the Baron's astonishment when among the persons of the Chief's entourage he recognized a man in native attire who whispered to him in English : " Don't betray me, I am here as a *hakim*," *i.e.* doctor. This mysterious personage was no other than Layard, then a young man and afterwards the famous explorer of Nineveh and our Ambassador at Constantinople. The Baron assisted him and lent him money. This I learnt much later from the Baron and from Sir Henry Austin Layard† himself,

---

* In 1829 the Russian Envoy and the whole Mission at Teheran were massacred. In 1836 it was the Baron's first duty to have his countrymen's mortal remains dug up and removed to a Christian burial ground.

† In reference to Layard, I may say that shortly before his death, more than 20 years ago, he encouraged me in my idea, which was also approved by Lord Salisbury, to build a railway from the Persian Gulf to Mohamarrah in Persia. The project was not realized because the British Government would grant no guarantee.

who spoke in grateful terms of my friend's kindness. This story shows the marvellous energy of Layard, who, without letters from the Shah or other assistance, had penetrated into the unruly land of the Bakhtiyaris, which no European had yet accomplished.

Perhaps the most interesting pages of de Bode's learned work, in which he first explored and explained the antiquities and curiosities of Persia, are consecrated to a description of the famous ruins of Persepolis—a host in itself. He says :—

I moved from one group of ruins to another like one under the influence of wine; my head felt quite giddy. Not that each separate monument was a masterpiece by itself: it was the *tout ensemble* which kept the mind and the imagination in a continued state of excitement. But these feelings, however delicious and grateful they might be to oneself, were yet so vague, so undefined, so confused even, that it would be impossible to bring them into any tangible form, for words are inadequate to give them expression.

I can only point out the elements which served to give birth to those feelings. It was the originality of the scene before me, so totally different from everything one is daily accustomed to meet; the chaste simplicity of the monuments. beautifully harmonizing with their gigantic proportions; the titanic rocks of marble and granite, evidently piled up with the presumptuous thought of struggling with Time as to who should have the mastery; and although nearly vanquished by the latter, the lofty columns still rearing their proud heads towards the skies.

The mystery attached to the origin and design of Persepolis; the isolated position it now occupies; the awful silence that it breathes around it; the generations of men and empires which have rolled over its head and sunk into oblivion; 'the events it has witnessed; the vicissitudes it has undergone; the noise and bustle of which once it must have been the centre, compared with the unearthly quiet which at present pervades its clustered pillars, were all fit subjects for meditation and capable of raising the soul above its ordinary level of indifference and apathy. Nor could the eye, while gazing on these memorials of past grandeur, help casting a look upward to the Throne of Omnipotence, where all was immutable and eternal. The pure, bright sky of the East, which had smiled upon the birth of Persepolis and witnessed its pristine glory, was the same which now looked down on its fallen grandeur—still pure, bright, and serene as the spirit which dwells there !

The author then enumerates the names of the learned travellers who visited Persepolis and observed the gradual destruction of the beautiful columns. In 1621 Pietro de la Valle found twenty-five columns standing, and in 1811 Sir W. Ouseley met only with fifteen columns.

The Baron refers to that marvellous work, "The History of the Caliph Vathek," due to the genius of Beckford, in which the mysterious subterranean passages of Takhti-Jemshid are described. The wonder is that Beckford himself never visited Persia, and that his marvellous tale, so true to life and to local scenery, was the brilliant creation of his own imagination and was actually written in a couple of nights.

"'Vathek,'" says Lord Byron, "was one of the tales I had a very early admiration of—for correctness of costume, beauty of description, and power of imagination, it far surpasses all European imitations, and bears such marks of originality that those who have visited the East will find some difficulty in believing it to be more than a translation. As an Eastern tale even Rasselas must bow before it; his 'Happy Valley' will not bear a comparison with the Hall of Eblis."*

While taking leave of the Baron's book we shall not part from him, for the following stray extracts from my diary testify that he and I travelled together :—

---

*William Beckford, the author of " Vathek," was one of the most remarkable men of modern times. He was the son of Alderman Beckford, of London, who bequeathed him property said to amount to upwards of £100,000 per annum. In a very few years he spent the enormous sum of £273,000 in erecting the much-talked-of Fonthill Abbey. An excellent scholar and possessed of a fine taste in almost every branch of art, he collected in the fantastic but costly "Abbey" one of the finest and most extensive libraries in England, and his pictures and curiosities were almost unequalled. His vast expenses and the loss of a large portion of his West Indian property rendered it necessary to sell his "Abbey" and collections in 1822. They fetched fabulous prices. Even catalogues were sold at a guinea each. He also wrote "Memoirs of Extraordinary Painters," and other works.

FROM RUSSIA TO PERSIA FIFTY YEARS AGO.

Now that Russia, Turkey and Persia are endowed with would-be or so-called constitutions, old notes of Oriental travel may perhaps have a semi-historical interest.

When residing at Tiflis and Bakou, in Transcaucasia, I went on two occasions to Persia with men who, in their younger days, had been prominent and popular diplomats in the Near East. Thanks to my travelling companions and to unbounded Russian hospitality and good nature I was received, both in Transcaucasia and in Persia, with every kindness by Russian as well as by English officials.

In the autumn of 1858 we started in a *tarantass* from Bakou, where raw naphtha was abundant but refined petroleum was yet unknown. We started for Lenkoran, near the River Astara. There we were provided with riding horses, as post-roads did not exist. Besides a Persian guide we had two Persian servants and two fine Cossacks. The weather was perfect, and as we ambled along the crisp, fine sand on the shore of the Caspian—with the sea on one side and beautiful forests on the other—I thought this mode of travelling approached as near perfection as anything my then youthful mind could imagine; I rather congratulated myself that there were no railways or even carriage-roads in Persia. Further on, however, we were warned to look out for quick-sands, in which some travellers had lately disappeared. We spent the night in a Persian hut, sleeping on carpets spread on the clay floor. From an open fire-place, with no chimney, the smoke issued through the room and escaped by a hole in the roof. There was no lack of rice, fowls, mutton and melons. Pomegranates, which grow in the surrounding woods, afforded pleasant drink instead of lemonade.

We soon reached Peri-Bazar and Enzeli, the harbour of Resht, in the Persian province of Ghilan. I have a vivid recollection of a road near Enzeli, which consisted of small ridges, with deep ruts on either side, formed by the hoofs of the numerous horses which had carried on pack-saddles the goods required by that locality. If your horse stepped on the hillock instead of the rut you might come down, horse and all.

Another two days of riding on wretched post-horses, some of which had wounds on their backs, brought us to some half-built and half-ruined Oriental so-called palaces. (Every new Shah builds new palaces, and does not finish those which his predecessors had commenced, for it is considered unlucky to do so.) Finally we reached the capital, whose streets were flanked with bare walls, as the windows looked out on interior courtyards or gardens, but some mosques and Government buildings could claim more pretension to architecture. The Russian Ambassador and his attachés came on horseback to meet my friend, and took us to their summer residence, called Zergende, where, among shady trees and a running stream, we were comfortably installed in a sort of bungalow.

The Ambassador, Mr. Anichkoff, was a clever diplomatist and a most entertaining and hospitable host, full of wit and humour, but a great *malade-imaginaire*. One of the younger attachés, Mr. Zinoviev,* was so light-haired that he looked almost like an albino. In later years he was himself the Russian Envoy in Persia, and concluded a treaty, which was much to the advantage of Russia. When Director of the Asiatic Department at St. Petersburg he signed, together with Sir West Ridgeway, the agreement about the frontier line after the Pendjeh incident. At the British Embassy Mr. Dorio (descendant of the Genoa Dorios) was at that time the Chargé d'Affaires, but he was laid up suffering from fever. With Mr. Thomson (later Sir Roland Thomson) and with the young, athletic doctor of the Embassy, Mr. Tollemache, I remember having a sharp ride along the stony country which surrounds Teheran.

Mr. Stevens, the Consul, was considered by the Russians as the moving spirit of the British Mission, and was suspected by the Russians of having brought about the war between England and Persia concerning Herat.

In Persia, as elsewhere, the country people, or rather the inhabitants of the mountains, are less corrupt and of a finer physique than the townspeople. Our guide, for instance, who had met us at the Russian frontier, was a mountaineer, and a finer looking man I have seldom seen.

The Persians are justly styled the Frenchmen of the East, as they are quick-witted and polite in their speech, apt to see the comical side of things, and desirous to turn people into ridicule. In the first half of the last century, Sir John McNeil, after having been the physician of the British Embassy at Teheran, returned home and came back again as Minister to replace Sir John Campbell. The Persian Master of the Ceremonies, before presenting the new Minister to the Shah, tried to make fun of the latter in the presence of the other foreign ambassadors by calling McNeil doctor, not ambassador, and asking him to look at his tongue, etc. But Sir John was equal to the occasion! After feeling the Khan's pulse the ex-physician told him, in the presence of the assembled diplomatists, that if he (the Khan) still persisted to drink rum at night it would ruin his health. To suggest that a Mussulman drank alcohol was to compromise his social position, and therefore no more efforts were made to make Sir John McNeil appear ridiculous.

In the way of books on Persia in those days, the travels of Jonas Hanway and Morier's " Hadji Baba of Ispahan " were among the most useful and entertaining.

---

* Later the Russian Ambassador at Constantinople.

My presentation to the Shah (the grandfather of the ex-Shah), who was then a handsome man of about 26 years of age, was on this wise : —

Having no uniform, I put on a black frock coat (a dress-coat, being open in front, is considered bad form in Persia) and wore an improvised white cap with a silver band. After walking through several courtyards or gardens with rose trees and fountains, and passing ante-rooms, some of which were decorated with theatrical representations of the Lion and the Sun, etc., we arrived at the door of the royal chamber, where the Master of the Ceremonies, an old Khan in a flowing silk dressing-gown and red leggings or stockings, told us to take off our over-shoes,* and to follow him. We saluted his Majesty three times with a military salute.

On another occasion we saw the Shah at Hamadan, the ancient *Ekbatana*, which is renowned for the tomb of the Biblical Mordecai, the Jew. We then walked through a field of narcissi. His Majesty was in a small square tent, one side of which was open. Some scrolls, and what looked like plans, were lying on the table. My old friend and myself were introduced by His Majesty's aide-de-camp, an Armenian, called Malkom Khan. It was said that this gentleman had influenced the Shah to become a Freemason, which was a bond of union between them. This young Armenian, Malkom Khan, whom I met many years later in London, where he was the Persian Ambassador, translated into perfect French the questions which his royal master addressed to us, and which referred to the former career of my friend and to a commercial enterprise which he wished to introduce in Persia. A comical side of this presentation was the appearance of Persian servants, among whom was a negro, all peeping out at us from behind the tent.

We presented a rifle and a watch to His Majesty, which were graciously accepted and acknowledged later on by conferring on us some decorations of the Lion and the Sun.

The presence of soldiers and other display of royal importance were theatrical and picturesque. On closer inspection most things, however, looked squalid, showing Oriental ignorance, mismanagement and official corruption.

Occasionally you saw a small group of gaudily-dressed horsemen with falcons and other Eastern attributes of sport and luxury belonging to the colonel of a regiment and his staff. At some distance you descried a few hundred men, some in uniform, others tattered and torn, followed by numerous stragglers—that represented a Persian regiment.

As regards trade, it may here be added that Russian, and especially German goods, were at that time few and far between in Persia, whereas

---

* Europeans, according to treaties, wear over-shoes, and slip them off, while natives take off their shoes or leggings, and enter the Shah's presence in their stockings.

calicoes, cutlery, sugar and other current articles of English manufacture predominated in all the bazaars of Persia. *Sic transit gloria mundi!* Now there are many more Russian and German than English goods in Persian bazaars.

In order to return to Tiflis we took another route, via Tabriz (or Tauris), the commercial capital of Persia, and the river Araxes, which is the frontier between Persia and Russia. We travelled slowly on our own riding horses, purchased at Teheran, with no small difficulty, as all the world had bought horses and followed the Shah to Hamadan.

At Tabriz, Mr. Tchernayev, the humorous Russian Consul, related an incident about an Armenian or Persian trader who had signed a bill of exchange, but would not pay the money when it fell due. The Consul asked him: Is that your signature? Yes. Do you owe the money to that man? Yes. Have you the means to pay? Yes. Then why don't you honour your draft? Bear with me, it does not pay me!

To describe Tabriz, the commercial capital of Persia, would be a work of supererogation, because, like every town in the East, it conveys the usual idea of a mass of heterogeneous structures, half-ruined, half-unfinished, with long bazaars, dirty eating and barbers' shops, mosques and baths. All life, as well as the countenances and dresses of the natives, are painfully uniform and monotonous. An appalling sight, which distresses a traveller on coming in or going out of a town, is the sight of miserable beings—probably lepers, covered with the most ghastly sores. They live in secluded mud huts and run after your horses, begging for alms.

Once again in Transcaucasia, we felt safer and more comfortable.

We left our riding horses and proceeded in a tarantass, swinging on long poles instead of springs. The post-stations had stoves, chairs, tables and more or less satisfactory food. At Erivan, which Field-Marshal Paskevitch (styled Prince Erivanski) had taken from the Turks at the beginning of the last century, we were lodged in the house of the Governor, General Koulubakin, as the latter had been a school-fellow of my fellow-traveller.

The General was an energetic man and a most original character. He was hot-headed, which had formerly brought him into collision with his chiefs.

On this journey our tarantass stuck in the snow, which lay in heavy masses near Mount Ararat and Lake Gokchi, where the Armenian Monastery of Etchmiazin is situated. Men and horses could not assist us, but fortunately a village, inhabited by a sect called Molokane, whose religious teaching is not unlike that of the Quakers, was in the neighbourhood. After waiting patiently iu the snow we saw a dozen stalwart men with large beards and broad wooden spades arrive on the scene. "Now we are all right," said my experienced friend, who knew the sterling qualities of these respectable peasants, and true enough we were soon dug out of the deep snow and again on the smooth road. This incident reminds me of what happened to us on another occasion at a post-station in Central Russia when we could not proceed for want of post-horses—a common dilemma when no railways existed. The obliging old post-master supplied us with tea and fish. Soon an open carriage drove up and out stepped a captain of the Imperial Navy. He looked very red and self-important. In a commanding tone he ordered horses. The post-master informed him that none were left in the stables. The excited traveller used hard names, with which the Russian vocabulary abounds, and wound up by stating that on the next day he would have the old post-master dismissed. Then turning to us he cried out: " And you, gentlemen, support this old rascal by drinking his tea and eating his fish while he pretends to be short of horses." My companion turned round and said: " When there are no horses, of which I have convinced myself by looking in the stables, it is wiser to drink tea than to make a disturbance." The officer now ordered in a peremptory tone that special horses should be procured from the peasants of the neighbouring village, adding that in a fortnight the post-master would be dismissed. Upon this the old man, knowing that he could only be dismissed by his own postal authorities, looked at us and said : "Observe, gentlemen, he has given me a reprieve of a whole fortnight." The post-master afterwards told us that this captain was one of the late so-called heroes of Sevastopol, who had lately been appointed Governor (gorodnichi) of the adjacent town of Efremoff.

After leaving the Caucasus and returning to Russia we were forcibly reminded that the country was as flat as the hand, consisting of plains, steppes, forests, and swamps, and that only the extremities and frontiers of the vast Empire were mountainous and picturesque, viz. : the Crimea, Transcaucasia, Finland, Podolia, parts of Poland, of Siberia, the Ourals, and Central Asia.

About a dozen years after my journey Mr. Augustus Mounsey, a Secretary of His British Majesty's Embassy, described the state of Persia much in the same dark colours as I have done. Bribery and corruption were as rampant as before. Persian morals had not improved.

Later, Dr. Wills, one of the officers of His Majesty's Telegraph Department, gave us his experiences as a physician in his book, " The Land of the Lion and the Sun." *Modakel* is the Persian word for perquisite or bribe. It is hopeless to fight against this system. The Persians from' the king downwards, all speak of *my modakel.* The governor of a province buys his appointment. I buy a horse, a carpet, or a pound of sugar, ten per cent. is added to my bill and paid to my servant. But more than ten per cent. is considered robbery.

Mr. Wills describes what he saw in the Persian capital :—

When we were in Teheran a number of Russian officers were engaged in forming so-called Cossack regiments. They engaged horsemen, whom they regularly paid, and seemed to be teaching these men their drill successfully. These so-called Cossacks were the Shah's favourite toy of the moment and he was never tired of reviewing them. They were well but plainly dressed, well horsed and well armed, and the Russian officers were very popular both with Shah and soldiers.

A large contingent of Austrian officers had also arrived to instruct the infantry and artillery. . . . The capital was ever a rather rowdy place ; murders and burglaries were common. . . . The police were so mercenary that the townspeople preferred being robbed to complaining to them, on the principle of two evils to choose the less.

The principal difficulty that the English merchant has to contend against is the difficulty he has *as an Englishman* to recover debts.

We want English consuls to protect us and our trade, say the merchants, and then the opening of the Kerūn river. Without these Persia as a mart is closed to English enterprise. We hope the Anglo-Russian *entente* has modified this state of things.

And now we come to the recent Anglo-Russian *entente,* dividing Persia into spheres of influence, which gave Russia more than a free hand in Persia†, where a nominal constitution was proclaimed in 1907. The Shah fled from Teheran to Odessa, where, it is said, he was allowed a pension of some twelve hundred pounds by Anglo-Russian arrangement.

The curious part of the business was that during the

---

† The larger and more important half, bordering on the Caspian, is Russia's sphere, and the smaller, the southern half, touching the Persian Gulf, is England's sphere ot influence.

insurrection in the streets of Teheran, the Shah (so he declared to a Russian newspaper correspondent) was left at the mercy of the insurgents by his own Cossack body-guard, commanded by a Cossack officer, who remained passive.

After his flight the Shah's son, a minor, was placed on the tottering throne under Russian tutelage, and the Shah himself was later heard of in a European watering-place.

Under the new dispensation the Persian Parliament requested the Government of the U.S.A. to recommend them an able financier to act as their Treasurer-General.

The activity of Mr. Morgan Shuster, who obtained this post, and the result of his endeavours, are the subject of an American book, entitled, "The Strangling of Persia," in which the American financier vindicates his conduct.

Says Mr. Shuster :—

The Mejilis (or Parliament) was remarkably expeditions in transacting business. It showed heated partisanship on some occasions, but older legislative institutions have not been free from this defect. While the Mejilis was not ideally representative in the political sense —that is, only a small proportion of the population had participated in the election of its members—it more truly represented the best aspirations of the Persians than any other body that had ever existed in that country.

On the other hand, a contemporary critic observes :—

It is interesting to know that the Russian Envoy offered Mr. Shuster Russian support if he would take office under the exiled Mahomet Ali, and it lends considerable colour to the idea that the Russian Government were not altogether ignorant of the movements of that ex-potentate. . . . It is useless in the circumstances to emphasize the rather too obvious fact that our cynical indifference to the fate of Persia is not likely to endear the British rule to our Mahommedan subjects elsewhere !

Mr. Shuster has been reproached with want of tact, but he did his best to protect Persian interests in an American business-like manner, which was not always pleasing to foreign diplomats, who desired that their Persian protégés should not be dunned to pay up taxes. There were also grasping Khans, who, instead of paying wages to soldiers, converted State money to their personal use.

The gendarmerie were wanted to protect the Treasury and the collection of taxes; therefore, a reliable English gentleman like Major Stokes, to whom, it was said,'Russian officials objected, was really necessary to command that corps. But he resigned.

Mr. Shuster thus concludes his denunciations against " The Strangling of Persia ":—

Persia's sole chance for self-redemption lay with the reform of her broken finances. . . .

The Persians themselves realised this, and with the exception of the corrupt grandees and dishonest public servants, all desired that we should succeed. Russia became aware of this feeling and unwittingly *paid us the compliment of fearing that we would not succeed in our task.* That she never intended to allow; all the rest of the controversy was detail.

Mr. Shuster shows Eastern women in a new and heroic light.

With the dark days when doubts came to be whispered as to whether the Mejilis (or Parliament) would stand firm, the Persian women, in their zeal for liberty and their ardent love for their country, threw down the last barriers which distinguished their sex and gave evidence of their patriotic courage. . . .

The President of the Mejilis consented to receive a. deputation of 300 women. In his reception-hall they confronted him, and, lest he and his colleagues should doubt their meaning, these cloistered Persian mothers, wives and daughters exhibited threateningly their revolvers, tore aside their veils, and confessed their decision to kill their own husbands and sons, and leave behind their own dead bodies, if the Deputies wavered in their duty to uphold the liberty and dignity of the Persian people and nation.

Though the Mejilis was destroyed by a *coup d'état* executed by Russian hirelings a week or two later, it passed out of being stainless of having sold its country's birthright.

Mr. Shuster was succeeded by a Belgian Treasurer-General, who has also been relieved of his functions by Russo-Persian arrangement.

As regards the actual situation of Persia, the following

declaration of the Russian Ambassador at Teheran, as reproduced by the *Westminster Gazette* of 18th March of this year, represents Russian policy.

(FROM OUR OWN CORRESPONDENT.)

BERLIN, March 16.—The Moscow *Russkoe Slovo* prints a long interview given to its Teheran correspondent by M. Korostovetz, the new Russian Minister. He develops a whole programme of policy as regards the Persian Constitution, armed forces, finances and railways; and also as regards the partial Russian occupation of the northern provinces; and he describes this policy as that of the Imperial Government, and not merely his own view of what is desirable.

M. Korostovetz says that Russia is friendly to the Constitution, and regards it as the only safeguard against anarchy and the only guarantee of the pushing through of reforms of the administration. Even in Russia's own interests the Constitution is essential. The British Government, the Minister makes out, is not so firm in the faith. Originally, he says, it stood for the Constitution, " but now, after experience, its attitude towards the Constitution is less optimistic, and it has ceased to be a warm supporter of the Constitution." Russian agents in Persia, says M. Korostovetz, have been ordered not to meddle in the Mejilis elections; but he adds further on that " the victory of the Left elements at the elections must not be tolerated, as a revolutionary Mejilis, unfriendly to the policy of Russia and England, might ruin the country and call forth a new catastrophe." The first two Mejilis did harm. " If the Left elements attempt again to play the leading rôle, Russia will intervene." A revision of the Constitution will probably be needed. The Cabinet must be given authority and solidarity.

He says that the position in Azerbeidjan is abnormal; but it is wrong to call the Governor, Sudja Dowla, a Russian tool. The Governor's merit is that he understood how to restore order, and realised that he could only do that by working with Russia. The people of Azerbeidjan do not want the Constitution; they will boycott the elections ; and Russia does not intend to force the Constitution on them. This will not prevent the convocation of the Mejilis. There is no possibility of the anti-Constitutionalist population wanting to secede. M. Korostovetz praises the Anglo-Russian agreement about Persia; and says that without it there would be no Persia to-day.

M. Korostovetz denies that Russia desires Persian territory ; and persists that the military occupation was " called forth by circumstances, not by the will of the Russian Government." A policy of complete evacuation is still the Russian ideal ; and it will be realised as soon as security is restored. On this point the Czar, the higher administration, and the Viceroy of the Caucasus are at one. It is untrue that the Russian troops will make elections impossible. " After the meeting of the Mejilis and the Shah's Coronation it will be best to evacuate Persia altogether."

The development taken by the Persian gendarmery is, says the Minister, causing anxiety to Russia. " Instead of protecting the routes, the gendarmery is becoming a real active army." This does not accord with Russia's interests. Russia will enter into negotiations with the Persian and British Governments in order to put precise limits to the development of the gendarmery. Russia has nothing to say against the increase of the gendarmery in the south ; but in the north the rôle of gendarme had best be left to the Persian Cossack Brigade; and the Persian Government must increase the number of Russian instructors in the brigade and increase the brigade's strength. Russia also desires that the police in the northern towns be reorganised by Russian instead of by Swedish instructors.

About the Trans-Persian railway he expresses doubt ; but in both Russian and Persian interests he favours the building of the proposed Astara-Teheran line. It is untrue, concludes M. Korostovetz, that Russia is unfriendly to the Persian Treasury and the Belgian officials, and it is untrue that the Russian immigrants in the north are being settled there with political aims.

Such was the report of the *Westminster Gazette's* correspondent at Berlin.

The grant of a Constitution to Persia called attention to that country, and Sir Mortimer Durand, formerly his Majesty's representative at Teheran, gave, some years ago (1907), an address in the Royal Asiatic Society.

He concluded by saying Persia was a country of great latent resources, with a quick-witted population, and she might yet again be a respectable Power with a voice in the councils of the world.

Recent Russian correspondents, writing from Persia, complain of German Consuls' overbearing preponderance, both in politics and trade, in the principal centres of Persia.

––––––––

Dr. POLLEN apologised for his late arrival, but he was detained on the road to the meeting ; otherwise he should have been there to have had the honour of presenting Mr. Cazalet as the lecturer. In that case he could only have repeated what he had often said as to the debt of gratitude the Society owed their President. They were on this occasion especially obliged to him for the manner in which he had prepared his most interesting paper. Mr. Cazalet had given them some vivid descriptions of his own personal experience in journeying through Persia in the *tarantass* and on the ambling nag. Dr. Pollen himself had some experience of that mode of travel and could certify as to the merits of locomotion on an ambling nag, to which our forefathers were so much devoted. In India, and especially in Sind, they trained steeds to adopt this pace by tying their legs together. Dr. Pollen then gave some of his own personal experiences of Persia, and told some tales about the King of Kings who declined to go to the Derby because he always knew that "one horse could run faster than another," and who dressed up the ladies of his harem on his return from London in ballet girls' dresses with bare legs and baby socks, and thus set a new fashion in Persia. The Persian woman, although she had a very narrow life behind the purdah, had more influence on public affairs in Persia than people imagined, as was proved by the fact mentioned by their President that when the purdah fell the Persian ladies could out-suffragette the British suffragette! The latter had not yet got to the stage of appearing before Parliament and producing revolvers and swords, and threatening to destroy their sons and husbands if they dared to sacrifice the true interests of their native land. Persia, said Dr. Pollen, had had a glorious past, and in spite of her miserable present there was no reason why she should not have a prosperous future. With reference to Mr. Cazalet's allusion to Persepolis, it was interesting to note that recent excavations, carried out under the patronage of Mr. Ratan Tata of Bombay, revealed the fact that 600 years before Christ, Persian influence extended to the banks of the Ganges, and under the modern city of Patna were to be found traces of the Palace of Chundra Gupta, which showed that it had been designed as an exact copy of the Palace and famous Audience Hall of Darius and his son Xerxes. Dr. Pollen then went on to hope that Persia would not become the victim of German culture, but the Emperor William had certainly designs on the Persian Gulf. Dr. Pollen recalled how he had, many years ago, written to the *Daily Mail* pointing out that the Kaiser's ambition really was to re-establish a Roman-German Empire, stretching from Holland through Vienna, Constantinople and Asia Minor to the shores of the Persian Gulf. England and Russia were bound to prevent the realization of this ambitious scheme of world predominance. Dr. Pollen begged to move a very hearty vote of thanks to Mr. Cazalet for all the trouble he constantly took for the good of the Anglo-Russian Literary Society, and especially for his paper that evening.

Dr. COUNSEL, in seconding the vote of thanks, congratulated the President and the Society upon his very interesting lecture, and his account of his personal travels. He reminded Members that Mr. Cazalet's distinguished uncle, Baron de Bode, was one of the authorities on Persian life and history, and that the published record of his travels, illustrated from his own sketches, is a work of great interest and of value as a work of reference. Dr. Counsel was able through the kindness of Miss Shippard to exhibit at the meeting a number of these original sketches in water-colour by Baron de Bode, as well as slippers and other interesting souvenirs of Persia, which he had presented to her family.

The vote of thanks was carried by acclamation.

LIFE AND WORK OF A. S. HOMIAKOV.

By FRANCIS P. MARCHANT.

Read by SKEETE WORKMAN.

IN the eighteenth century Kiril Ivanovitch Homiakov, of advanced years, possessed vast property consisting of the village Boutcharovo, in Tula government, estates in Riazan, and a house at St. Petersburg. Concerned lest his wealth should pass into wrong hands after his death, he invited the *mir* to elect a successor, stipulating that he should be a member of the Homiakov family. A young sergeant of the Guards, Fedor Stepanovitch Homiakov, was elected with the approval of Kiril Ivanovitch, and his management of the estate proved excellent. When in 1787 the Tsaritsa Elizabeth passed through Tula she advised the nobility to open a bank, but they said this was unnecessary as Fedor Stepanovitch was virtually the banker. His son Alexander dissipated the estates, and his grandson Stepan further embarrassed them by gaming, and transferred them to his wife (*née* Maria Kireievska). Their second son, Alexis, the subject of this study, was born at Moscow on May 1st, 1804. During the stormy times of 1812–13 the family took keen part and interest in the affairs of the country and its activities, showing greater zeal than many other families of good position. An ancestor, Peter Semenovitch, had been a falconer to the Tsar Alexis Mikhailovitch, and the family archives contained letters from the Tsar.

The young Alexis was a diligent learner of German, French, English, and Latin, passing afterwards to Greek

and Sanscrit. Discovering a misprint in a copy of a Papal
bull printed in a book, he proceeded to express doubts of
Papal infallibility to his tutor, Abbé Boivin, and was
chastised for this precocity. Alexis and his brother
dreamed of fighting Napoleon, and on hearing of Waterloo
Fedor asked, " Whom shall we fight now?" Alexis declared
" I will stir up the Slavs." The dramatist Gendre, a friend
of Griboiedov, was their tutor for Russian literature;
Dr. Glagolev taught them and Dmitri and Alexis Venevitinov
philosophy ; mathematics was learnt from Professor
Shtshepkin. At fifteen, Alexis Homiakov translated the
" Germania" of Tacitus, his work appearing in the Trans-
actions of the Society of Lovers of Russian Literature. The
War of Greek Independence fired the ardour of the youthful
Alexis, whose family were friends with Count Capo d'Istria.
Providing himself with a false passport, a knife, and fifty
roubles, he set out from home one evening; his father
organised pursuit and he was brought back but not punished,
while Fedor was reprimanded for not restraining his junior
brother. In due course Alexis enlisted in the Cuirassiers
and afterwards in the Horse Guards. Among his friends of
youth were his cousin V. S. Kireievsky, I. V. Kireievsky,
A. A. Mukhanov, and A. I. Koshelev, and Dmitri Venevitinov
was the centre of the group. The bonds of union of the
friends were German philosophy and Western ideals, but
young Homiakov and P. V. Kireievsky were united in zeal
for the development of an independent Russia.

The young cornet of Guards came in touch with the
Dekabristi, and argued with Ryleiev that forces armed for
the defence of the nation had no right to settle the destinies
of the nation at their will. Fedor Stepanovitch being
engaged at the Paris Embassy, Alexis obtained permission
to visit him there, but meanwhile his brother was transferred
to St. Petersburg. He stayed in Paris for a year and a half.

Being short of money temporarily, Alexis painted a picture for a Roman Catholic church—an uncongenial task for a Slav—which he relinquished on receiving a remittance from home. From Paris he proceeded to Switzerland, Northern Italy, and through Western Slav countries to Russia. Architecture attracted his attention, and he came to the conclusion that its source was religion and that its beginning was to be sought for in the East—in India and Egypt —and not among the imitators of the Romans. Alexis returned to Russia at the end of 1826, and pursued his artistic activities at the Hermitage. Fedor Homiakov, on the outbreak of war with Turkey, was attached to the staff of Paskievitch in the Caucasus and soon died there. Alexis went to the Danube and served as adjutant to General Prince Madatov, and was decorated for valour at Shumla and Bazardzhik. After the war he returned to Moscow. Rejoining his former circle of friends, he became an ardent partisan of an independent Russia as against the Schelling and Hegel groups, but his voice appeared as if crying in the wilderness. His uncle, S. A. Kireievsky, sickened and died in 1836, and in that year Alexis became engaged to Katerina Mikhailovna Yazikova, sister of the poet N. M. Yazikov, the bridegroom being thirty-two and the bride eighteen. Thanks to the high moral standard instilled into him by his mother, Alexis proved an excellent husband and father. Two sons were born but soon died, but later they had five daughters and two sons in all. The life was divided between Moscow and the country estates which, as a sportsman, Alexis liked to visit in spring and autumn. His mother, with advancing years, became rather a trial, with incessant grief for her eldest son, needless reproaches about mismanagement, and Alexis' —to her mind—Liberal and Protestant tendencies. She died in July, 1857. In 1847, Alexis Homiakov, with his wife and two eldest children, set out for foreign travel, visiting Germany, England, France, and Bohemia. At Prague, soon to be the centre of the Slavic Congress and a national movement, he met Hanka, librarian and man of letters, famous in connection with the Kralodvorsky manuscripts. Of England, he said that he arrived there with cheerful astonishment, and left with a melancholy love.

Homiakov and his friends came to be known as Slavianophils, and he wrote that this name, given derisively, founded on foreign analogy, which in Russian ought to be *Slavianoliubtsy* (lovers of the Slavs) was quite acceptable to them. Every Russian should be a Slavophil. Evidence could be found among Russian soldiers in the Turkish war or on the Moscow *Gostinny dvor*, where Frenchmen, Germans, and Italians were regarded as foreigners, while Serbs, Dalmatians, and Bulgars were brethren. Count S. G. Stroganov was not in favour of the Slavophils, and all kinds of restrictions were set up against them. The wearing of beards and distinctively Russian dress provoked persecution, and many sympathisers held aloof. 'The Clergy, generally speaking, including the Metropolitan Philaret, regarded the movement doubtfully, as Homiakov found when he attempted to further relations between the Orthodox and Anglican Churches. After the death of the Tsar Nicholas, the Slavophils breathed more freely.

The activities of Alexis Stepanovitch were many-sided. He was a landed proprietor, artist, sportsman, and man of letters; he devised a successful remedy for cholera, sent a rifle to the Ministry of War, and a steam-engine to a London exhibition, which he called the Moskowka Rotatory Steam-engine. The emancipation problem engaged his attention. S. T. Aksakov said: " Out of Homiakov could be made ten men, each one better than he." With all his industry he had a reputation for laziness. He enjoyed good health, except for attacks of eye-trouble and typhus. This latter complaint carried off his beloved wife at Moscow in January, 1852, a calamity which he considered as a call to sustained and serious work. In his grief the dying Zhukovsky sent Alexis his blessing. The death of Gogol was a heavy blow, as was that of the philosopher I. V. Kireievsky, and gradually the circle dwindled. On September 23rd, 1860, at Ivanovskoye, his Riazan estate, Alexis Stepanovitch passed away through cholera, attended by his friend L. M. Muromtsev. " I have cured many and cannot cure myself," were his words of Christian resignation to the last summons. Homiakov reposes in the Danilov monastery at Moscow by the side of his wife, and on monuments around are the names of Prince Tsherkassky, Gogol, Yazikov, Valuev, Samarin, and other friends. His biography, with a summary of his views, has been written by Mr. Valerian Liaskovsky, and we are much indebted to this work for the foregoing facts.

The works of A. S. Homiakov have been published in four volumes, of which the second edition is before us. The first volume, consisting of numerous articles, was edited after his death by J. S. Aksakov in 1861. It is quite impracticable to examine all in detail, but we shall endeavour to furnish as complete an idea as possible of the workings of that cultured, catholic mind. In the first article, on views of foreigners about Russia, he shows how a Russian traveller returning home tells his stay-at-home friends what a wonderful book Lord ——, Marquis ——, bookseller ——, Dr. ——, has written about Russia ; though there is much nonsense there is great truth. The stay-at-home buys the wonderful work and finds how full of ignorance and prejudice it is. "It is strange that Russia alone has, as it were, the privilege of arousing the worst feelings of the European heart." We do not know Russia; a man cannot know his own face without a mirror, and he has not invented a mental mirror to reveal his spiritual and moral physiognomy; it is equally difficult for a nation to know itself. He considers West European nations as being under formalism—cold calculation—with a tincture of national and personal pride lightly modified by some " half-vicious virtues," including England in her external policy.

But not internal England, full of spiritual life and power, full of reason and love; not England of election majorities, but of harmony in judgment of men bound by oath; not savage England covered with baronial castles, but spiritual England, which does not allow bishops to fortify their dwellings; not England of the East India Company, but England of the missionaries; not England of the Pitts but of the Wilberforces, England wherein there is still tradition, poetry, sanctity of home life, warmth of heart, and Dickens, younger brother of our Gogol; in fact, Shakespeare's merry old England.

The vices of the French language have belonged to all European languages more or less, but the great Russian nation speaks its own literary language and perhaps even better than its literature. In the second article, on views of Russians about foreigners, he gives with approval a shrewd French observation :—

Vous autres Russes, vous me paraissez un singulier peuple; enfans de noble race, vous vous amusez à jouer le rôle d'enfans trouvés.

He also approves of d'Israeli's remark, " English manners save England from English laws." To be a Russian (" On the possibility of a Russian artistic school ") it is not enough to know Russian grammatically, statistics, and to study literary memorials; in that way one could be a respectable Russist (like a Hellenist, Latinist, &c.), but never a living Russian man. Perhaps love of Russia exists among us, says Homiakov, but it is like the good Englishmen's love for negroes, Hottentots and Indians, with a conviction of mental and moral superiority and the hope of a rôle of future if not present benefactors. However, the fine invisible cords uniting the Russian soul to his country and nation are not subject to reasoning analysis. A Russian song cannot be proved to be better than an Italian barcarolle or tarantella, but it appeals more deeply to the Russian heart and ear. An attack on Russian dress is an attack on freedom of taste and feeling, and rejection of Russian garments as Russian seems strange and somewhat of an insult.

Of especial interest to us all must be his "Letter on England," visited in 1847, when Gogol saw him off at Ostend, "You'll like our old England," said one of the steamer crew, an exact prophecy. The quiet of the English Sunday greatly impressed our traveller, who had no patience with those who disliked and misunderstood it. He extols our hospitality, and if we do not readily open our doors we treat the guest well. "The soul wearied of the serious materialism of Germany and the smiling materialism of France breathes freely in England, and at the same time permits itself to laugh at her Dombeys and at the travellers who can see nothing but Dombeys there." Every English-man is in fact a Tory at heart. "English history is not a thing of the past for the modern Englishman: it lives throughout his life, in all his customs, in almost every detail of his life." The Englishman wanders in Westmin-ster Abbey with a deep, sincere, and ennobling love, and esteems the law, because the English law is so completely English. Homiakov's remarks on Oxford and Cambridge and their place in English life evince keen insight. Oxford is more charming than Venice, with its luxury and delicacy, for over Oxford hovers a severe and resplendent soul. The chief basis of English life is certainly religion, as hundreds of missionaries and preachers are the outward expression of a common spirit and tendency. Reverent worshippers in churches, street crowds listening to a poor old man expounding (if feebly) texts of Scripture, and knots of work-men engaged in theological arguments on Sunday, remind him of holy, devout Russia. (We cannot help wondering what Homiakov would have made of cultured and not irreverent scepticism, represented by Matthew Arnold, Lecky, and Huxley.) The Englishman recalls the Russian in a pro-found and real distrust of human reason. He had an amusing chat with a lawyer, who said: "We are, sir, the plague of our country, and in studying our history I cannot blame Cade and Tyler for hanging us." Among Englishmen, ignorance of the simplest facts is united with a sound and lofty comprehension of spiritual principles. Outside England, Tory principles are represented in Russia by the Kremlin, the caves of Kiev, the Solovetsky Mon-astery, sanctity of family life, and predominant Orthodoxy. In conclusion, he says that England will not perish, which has done so much for Christianity, but he fears the "Protestant axe," and demands a new spiritual principle to save us. To have read no more than this magnificent letter is to lay us under a great obligation to A. S. Homiakov.

In an essay on "Aristotle and a Universal Exhibition," he says that Peter the Great performed no little service to the country, and became the Russian Aristotle; but the country should free itself from the occidental life which he introduced and give up the *magister dixit*. There is more admiration of England in this essay, and of her love of antiquity, while Homiakov is struck with the Crystal Palace. At the same time he finds nothing more amusing than a Russian Anglomaniac. In criticising an article of I. V. Kireievsky on European and Russian culture, he disagrees with the view that Christian doctrine was ex-pressed in all its fullness and purity in the public and private life of Ancient Russia, and asks when this occurred. In spite of his love for his country he could not make such an assertion, for with Christianity began the development of Russian life. All the Western nations stood in a far worse relation to Christianity than Russia, which had one source of enlightenment—Faith. The Metropolitan Alexis and St. Sergius did more for the unity of the Russian land than the cunning policy of Simeons, Dmitris, and Ioanns. Writing on modern philosophical phenomena, Homiakov calls Hegel the fullest and even the only rationalist in the world. In an argument on personal evidence of the existence of St. Peter's, he reduces Hegel to this *reductio ad absurdum*, "for him Prussia is the actual cause of Egyptian or Greek history, and by no means in a teleological sense." In the essay on "The Old and the New," Homiakov has no sympathy with those who lament the "good old times;" we know contemporary Russia, but must guess out old Russia. There is a good summary of Peter the Great's activity, who came as a terrible and yet beneficent shock to his countrymen, disturbing robber-judges, nobles who thought of their rank and not of the country, monks who sought personal salvation in cells and collections in cities and forgot the Church, humanity and Christian brotherhood. There are accounts of Ivan the Terrible, a stranger to human love, and his son Feodor, whose reign was one of happiness to Russia, he says, while too much credit is given for good results to the wisdom of Boris Godunov. The Orthodox world (Glinka's " Life for the Tsar ") is one of song, and discourse itself in songs is most natural. Literature and music have grand exemplars in Gogol and Glinka.

The sportsman comes out in an article on sport and hunting. The learned and sedate Germans cannot understand the English love of sport, and that a wise nation can indulge in such triviality. He quotes newspaper accounts of hunting performances by Lords Fitzhardinge and Gifford,

and goes on to discuss breeds of dogs. Homiakov's opinion
of the Norman Conquest and its effects on the Anglo-Saxon
world (instead of a preface to Valuev's writings) is scarcely
just, and though there may be reasons for deploring this
important fact in our history, the Normans were not as
inhuman and depraved as he seems to think. " The Slavonic
world holds for humanity, if not the germ, then the possibility
of regeneration." His historical writings brought him into
conflict with Professor Granovsky. He does not like our
erratic English alphabet, while Cyrillic is a reasonable one.
" A Chat at Podmoskovna " of two ladies and two gentlemen
is full of interesting reflections. Tulnev is not altogether
correct when he says that there is no question of nationality
in England or France since there are no foreign elements
there: admitting the latter fact, " home rule " aspirations,
especially with ourselves, must not be overlooked. Zaputin
truthfully says—of the Russian of those days at all events—
that " we belong far less to our nationality than educated
Englishmen, French, or Germans to their own." Homiàkov
writes in glowing terms of Lord Metcalfe, Governor-
General of East India, Jamaica, and Canada, " a pre-
eminently Christian official," who brought honour to
his country and who belongs to the whole of humanity.
" Such men as Wellington, Collingwood, Bentinck, and
Metcalfe are the strength of England." We seem to hear
L. N. Tolstoy in Homiakov's letter to T. I. Philippov, when,
in a discussion of family love, he says that for some men
natural and necessarily limited family love would militate
against love of humanity in general. " That which elevates
average people might be an occasion of falling to the
highest. The family itself would be a hindrance to their love
of humanity." Such considerations, which have influenced
saints of many religions, obviously do not appeal to the vast
majority of Christians, and Alexis Stepanovitch was a model

husband and father, while not unmindful of the duty to love his neighbour as himself. It is remarkable to find a eulogy of Voltaire, " more of a Christian than his antagonists," *e.g.*, in the Calas and other affairs. " Voltaire employed against false Christianity of his time a weapon derived from Christian truth." Writing on juridical questions, he says, " to us, by the grace of God, has been granted Christianity in all its purity, in all its reality of brotherly love. . . . Russia must be either the most moral, *i.e.*, the most Christian, of all human societies, or nothing at all." Finally, for we must refrain from further citations, a speech at a meeting of the Society of the Lovers of Literature, in 1859, is a magnificent tribute to the influence of Moscow in Russia. " The Moscow word has become the common Russian word. . . . There, we may say, is constantly worked out the thought of Russian society of to-morrow . . . we may say of thought in Moscow what Dante says about the eyes of one of the heroic figures of his poem : *gli occhi nel muover onesti e tardi.* Such eyes and such movement of thought please me." It was only right and proper, he thought, that such a society should be formed at Moscow.

The second volume, with a portrait of A. S. Homiakov for frontispiece, is taken up with theological writings, with a preface by Y. F. Samarin written in 1867. He says that these are the most important, most complete, and yet the least known of his works. A remark of Homiakov quoted is that " for science is necessary not only freedom of opinion but also freedom of doubt." Science, says Samarin, is related more directly with Latin and Protestant Christianity than with Orthodoxy. Homiakov was one of the lights of the rich Pushkin Pleiades, but he lacked artistic talent. He was theologian, mechanician, philosopher, engineer, philologist, doctor—a master, connoisseur, and inventor, said his friends, though opponents called him a dilettante in everything. " He lived in the Church," says Samarin, and proceeds to explain what is meant: .the Church is the manifestation on earth of unadulterated truth and inviolable right. Wherever he was, Homiakov observed the fasts. He thought that tradition ought not to fetter the progress of science —a recurrent problem for the earnest inquirer. " Homiakov first looked upon Latinism and Protestantism *from within* the Church, consequently *from above*." His one theme is, " the Church as a living organism of truth entrusted to mutual love ; or, as freedom in unity and unity in freedom; or, as freedom in the harmony of its manifestations." Samarin concludes—Homiakov is a teacher of the Church.

To analyse the series of essays is beyond our power. Homiakov thoroughly understands the points of view of all branches of the Christian Church, whether those of highly developed systems of doctrine and ritual, or those of primitive and simple ideals. He examined the writings of Vinet, a learned French Protestant, the Biblical labours of Bunsen, the Jansenist Looss, and the Jesuit Father Gagarin. His signature for theological articles was " Ignotus." We may gather fine gems of thought : " Love is the crown and glory of the Church"; " Contempt for the body is the sin of spiritual pride." The name *Pravoslavia* will disappear when all branches of the Church are united in truth. Homiakov does not approve of Anglicanism, and thinks it will follow Gallicanism. He had a long correspondence in English with the Rev. W. Palmer and the Rev. G. Williams. The former translated some of Homiakov's verses, which led to friendly relations. In one of his letters to Palmer he refers to the death of his wife, who asked if they could praise God in the same Church with Palmer and Williams. He was familiar with the Gorham controversy and judgment. Translations of Pauline epistles are included in this volume.

The third volume contains writings on universal history, with a preface by the eminent scholar and traveller, A. F. Hilferding, dated March, 1872, who says that Homiakov was apparently desirous of composing some magnificent and solid work of erudition besides poems and articles. One day Gogol surprised him writing, caught sight of the name of Semiramis, and spread it about that Alexis Stepanovitch was writing a *Semiramide*. Friends began to ask when the *Semiramide* would be ready, and he replied: "Not in my lifetime; after my death perhaps some one will issue it." This is what actually happened, and these chapters form the " Semiramide," which he began about 1838. The author had not arranged his materials into form, and his editor had great difficulty in devising some kind of system, since all depended on Homiakov's wide reading and prodigious memory, without notes or references to originals and authorities. It is not, says Hilferding, a narrative universal history, but a scheme of how history should be related. Homiakov never discussed it with his friends, as was his usual habit when he had literary work in hand. He was at a disadvantage in that knowledge of Slavonic antiquities, the scientific study of which had not long begun, had been mingled with fantastic theories. For example, Shafarik's famous work opened up a wide and interesting field, but Kollar's poems were those of an ardent dreamer. In consequence, Homiakov held exaggerated views of the importance and extent of the ancient Slav. We glance through page after page of antiquities, history, mythology, and philology, but since Homiakov studied and wrote much has been abandoned and knowledge has been entirely recast. These remarks apply to the fourth volume of Homiakov's works, which Hilferding did not live to see published. Notes " by the editor " prove the conscientious care with which a busy scholar arranged the manuscript of a beloved teacher, and, as a brief foreword explains, the edition serves as a memorial of both.

There remains the poetry of the great Slavophil, some of which has been rendered into English.* His first effusion was " Desire for Quiet," written at Petrograd in 1824, in which the bard felt the call in the blood, the enthusiasms to ripen into thought and action. In " Youth " he is like a future Titan who would seize Nature in a passionate embrace, though in " Two Hours ' he refers to the poet's dark hour, when inspiration is lacking, no rays shine through the gloom, and Phœbus is mean. There is a prophetic ring about " Approaching Sleep," a prayer that when the Angel of Death comes Homiakov might receive him as a long-expected guest, with fearless eye, and soul released from mist and gloom to enjoy a brilliant flight. In " An Ode " Homiakov evokes maledictions of the future on him whose voice commanded him to serve against Slavs (*i.e.*, the Poles, in the troubles of 1830), and on past traditions, vanished deceits, and stories of vengeance and suffering; the inspired bard sees the Slav eagles arise and break into broad, daring flight, but bowing before the oldest —the Eagle of the North. " The Eagle " is a magnificent expression of the Slav idea ; the eagle flying in the heavens must not forget his little brothers of the Danube, Alps, Carpathians and Balkans. Like other young men of his time, Homiakov was taken with Mdlle. A. O. Rossetti, but when he talked to her of Russia and endeavoured to interest her in national songs he met with chilling indifference. In " To my Children " he commemorates two sons of feeble health, lost in 1838. Moreover, Homiakov was a writer of deep, spiritual poetry, as, for example, the verses on the duty

---

*An earlier number of our *Proceedings* contained the lecturer's version of " To the Slav Cities." Dr. J. Pollen's " Russia Repentant " appears in No. 70, p. 92.

of a singer-pastor whose warfare is not with carnal but spiritual weapons, not with the armour and sword of Saul but with the Word of God; other verses are in the nature of a warning against spiritual pride : God is not with those who cry, "We are the salt of the earth, the pillars of the Temple, the shield and sword of God." A call for the slumbering brother to midnight prayer breathes a devotional spirit. In "Russia" the poet sings of her glorious destiny; where are Rome and the Mongols? Pride must not be indulged in, although God has blessed Russia and intended her for an example to other nations. Homiakov's sense of brotherhood and appeals to the fraternal spirit shine through the verses on Easter morning service at the Kremlin. The Crimean War could not fail to exercise the patriotic Muse, but one effusion—a call to humility and repentance— rendered him unpopular in Moscow. Indeed, no preacher who indicates weakness and faults can expect to escape hostility.

We take leave of Alexis Stepanovitch Homiakov by a rendering of the album verse written at Prague for Vaclav Hanka, the man of letters and librarian celebrated in the Kralodvorsky (Königinhof) manuscripts controversy, whose Slavonic zeal probably outran his discretion :—

At one time I prayed God about Russia, and said :—
Remove from her all slavish dulness,
Preserve her from a pride that's blind,
Infuse in her a living fullness
To cheer a dying, doubting mind !

This is my prayer for all the Slavs. As long as no doubt is ours there will be success. There is power in us as long as brotherhood is not forgotten. It will always be a sincere happiness for me to remember that I was enabled to write this in your book.

The Chairman proposed a very hearty vote of thanks to the author and to the reader of the excellent paper.

He commended Mr. Marchant's ability, industry and whole-hearted devotion to the A.R.L.S. Mr. Cazalet likewise observed that Mr. A. S. Homiakov was not only a great Slavophil and a poet who raised the ideals of morality and patriotism among his countrymen but he was also an Anglophil, for he sympathised with our British institutions. What further endeared his memory to the A.R.L.S. was that Mr. Homiakov's worthy son, an ex-President of the Duma, was a distinguished Member of our Society for the last 20 years. Mr. Cazalet recommended the members of the A.R.L.S. to read once more in our *Proceedings* Dr. Pollen's translations of Homiakov and other Russian poets. Dr. Pollen was himself a poet, and sometimes even improved on the originals. This was not a compliment but a fact.

DR. POLLEN, in seconding the vote of thanks to Mr. Marchant and to Mr. Workman, said the paper had been well composed and beautifully and clearly read. It was a pleasure to listen to it, and he felt the vote of thanks was carried already.

Dr. Pollen drew attention to the appeal, in a recent leading article in the *Morning Post*, to all those who knew and understood Russia to come forward and enlighten the British public as to the true nature of the Russian people and the Russian administration.

Russia was once more rendering heroic services to the Western World and to the cause of civilization. Homiakov had celebrated Russia as " Russia Repentant," after the Crimean War, and Mr. Cazalet had alluded in the most gratifying manner to his (Dr. Pollen's) translation of that poem. There could be no doubt that Homiakov was a very able and very far-seeing man, and he foretold the coming greatness of his Fatherland. He made some mistakes in estimating foreign nations, and he was certainly wrong in thinking the English were at heart Tories. "Tories," as they knew, were originally a tribe of Irish robbers who posed as Government officials and plundered with impunity. Mr. Marchant apparently gave Homiakov credit for understanding all Christian Churches. If Homiakov really did do this, he must have been a very clever man indeed.

He, no doubt, understood the Russian people and their marvellous faith, their realising sense of the unseen, and their consequent devotion to their religion. They were a most religious people, and would remain religious to the end. Some said they were superstitious, but better to be that than have no religion at all.

As to what Homiakov said about lawyers being a plague, Dr. Pollen thought Homiakov was about right.

Although, in point of fact, a lawyer himself, Dr. Pollen thought that the less people had to do with lawyers the better. The Lords, the Lawyers, and the Levites often proved too much for any man, and they were certainly a most dangerous combination. The three "L's" proved too much even for Cromwell, but the most formidable of the L's were undoubtedly the lawyers. Dr. Pollen had much pleasure in seconding the vote of thanks which Mr. Cazalet had so ably proposed.

The vote was carried unanimously by the appreciative audience.

REVIEWS OF BOOKS, Etc.

ENGLISH CHURCH WAYS.

By W. H. FRERE, D.D. (Murray, 1914.)

THE objects of these lectures, which are connected with the Anglican and Eastern-Orthodox Churches and the Russian Society for promoting a *rapprochement*, have found an eloquent exponent in the Rev. W. H. Frere, who addressed a mixed audience of Russians and English residents at St. Petersburg.

The lectures were translated, sentence by sentence, into Russian by Mr. N. Lodygensky, who, together with Mme. Alexeieff and Mr. P. Mansouroff, is the heart and centre of the Russian movement, to advance the *Union of the Churches*.

These efforts are especially interesting at the present time, for from the St. Petersburg Press and other sources of information we learn that the Eastern Church is in a state of transition. Russians of various classes and for different reasons criticise the organization of their Mother Church. Another vexed question is whether only monks and not priests are to be raised to bishoprics. Among the *intelligenzia* and others agnosticism is on the increase. The Anglican Church could scarcely be understood and appreciated by the rank and file of the Russian nation.

Undenominational evangelisation, as practised by English Baptists and their friends in Russia, has met with considerable success, for among the peasantry there is a craving for the religion of the heart to replace the formalism of the official Church !

The number of dissenters and sects is a proof in point, and some are the best representatives of the Slav race.

A Russian priest in London approved of the projected union, but suggested that the Anglican Church should be *annexed* by the Eastern-Orthodox Church!

In religious matters and in social questions an important factor is an intimate knowledge of the people's characteristics. From Trufanoff, alias Hiliodare Rasputin, the Siberian, down to the so-called Saint Innocent of Balta (see A.R.L.S.'s No. 69), many exploit the credulity of men and women, high and low, and continue to exercise a certain influence on the masses in Russia.

Under these circumstances, while admiring the noble aim and the eloquent pleading of the Reverend author, we fear that the practical realisation of his religious scheme can scarcely be achieved. It may, however, dissolve some Russian misunderstandings about " our bustling English ways in religion," as the author puts it. A. S. Homiakov, as may be seen from the lecture earlier in this number, thoroughly knew all aspects of the question.

We subjoin a Notice of the

ANGLICAN AND EASTERN-ORTHODOX CHURCHES UNION.

This Union was founded in 1906 to promote the cause of better relations and ultimately of the restoration of Intercommunion between the Anglican and Eastern-Orthodox Churches, of which the Russian is chief in point of numbers and power. It works by means of mutual intercourse and co-operation, and by methods of bringing about a better mutual understanding, such as lectures, visits and literature. Its work is thus in the religious world parallel to that of the Anglo-Russian Literary Society, and will appeal to many of the members of the latter.

The Orthodox President is the eminent Archbishop Agathangel of Yaroslaff, and it has among its members Archbishop Evlogie of Volhynia. It numbers now about 2,060 members in all parts of the world, and has a powerful branch in the United States. A striking advance was the formation in 1912 of the sister Society with similar objects in Russia, under the sanction of the Holy Synod, of which Archbishop Sergie of

Viborg is President. Many lectures are given on the Orthodox Church in England, and two lecturers, English Priests, have visited Petrograd at the invitation of the Russian Society, to give lectures on the English Church doctrine and life.

The General Secretary, the Rev. H. J. Fynes-Clinton, 27, Finsbury Square, E.C., would be glad to give further particulars of the Society.

COUNT LORIS-MELIKHOV'S CONSTITUTION AND HIS PRIVATE LETTERS.

(IN RUSSIAN.)

(H. Steinetz, Berlin.)

LORIS-MELIKHOV was an able Russian general and an enlightened statesman, about whose remarkable career little is known in England. An Armenian by origin, his younger days were spent in successful warfare in the Caucasus against the Circassians, and with Turkey. Later he occupied various high administrative posts (Governor-General of Kharkov, &c.), and was so much appreciated by Alexander II. that he became Minister of the Interior, and practically dictator.

The Count's draft of a constitution would have been adopted had the best of Czars not been murdered. A constitution might have prevented the outbreak of the smouldering revolution. It was calculated to re-organise the civil and military administration, to expand local government, to improve education, to give freedom to the press, and to grant the people the right to participate in the control of the country.

After Loris-Melikhov's death, which occurred in Paris, a secretary of the Russian Embassy affixed seals on his documents and letters, but copies of these papers had been confided to a friend, who is now deceased.

The Russian book under our consideration also refers to the Count's earlier career. When in 1877-8 he defeated the Turks at Kars, the Imperial Viceroy of the Caucasus, prompted by jealous satellites, came to the seat of war in order to let them reap the credit of the campaign, and conferred the St. George's Cross (corresponding to our V.C.) on a member of his own staff who had taken no part in the military operations.

The question of a constitution was a natural sequence of the emancipation of the serfs in 1862. It had long been *sur le tapis*, for there was seething discontent in the nihilistic *intelligenzia*, and poverty among the ignorant peasantry, partly in consequence of the dishonesty and maladministration of officials, all of which caused anxiety to the benevolent monarch.

On the untimely death of Alexander II., a majority of two votes in the Council of Ministers disapproved of Loris-Melikhov's Constitution, and it was abandoned, to the satisfaction of Alexander III., who is said to have observed to his brother the Grand Duke Vladimir, " a mountain off my shoulders."

Although Alexander III. followed the counsels of Pobedonostsev to leave matters in *statu quo*, suggestions about constitutional changes came from various quarters: the old Emperor of Germany, the head of the French police, Monsieur Andrieu, the pseudo-liberal professor of Moscow University, Mr. Chicherin, and others, in various walks of life, volunteered their advice, but nothing came of it all.

Suspicions were aroused by Katkov, the editor of the *Moscow Vedomeste*, against the loyalty of personages in high positions, including the Grand Duke Constantine, the uncle of the Czar. A character sketch by Prince G. Volhonsky precedes some extracts from Count Loris-Melikhov's private letters, addressed to a person whose name is not given :

They (his enemies) want to catch some trivial gossip and to expand it in order to make political capital. A sorry and a silly game.

His private fortune was meagre, for public business had absorbed all his attention.

In one of the letters the Count, writing about current politics, expresses regret at the murder of Cavendish and Burke in Phœnix Park, and praises Gladstone for being well disposed to Russia.

ARMY STORIES AND SKETCHES. (Russian.)

By Egor Egorov. (Berisovski, St. Petersburg.)

THE author exposes the short-comings of the Army through the medium of short stories.

This *modus operandi* was mostly used by writers of the last century, when censors were more repressive than now.

Some of the scenes and conversations are amusing, but the triviality ascribed to officers is scarcely credible. The French word *niaiserie* might best define their talk and actions. In some cases the officers' wives are the ruling spirits of the regiment, while reckless expenditure brings ruin to many. Abuses in hospitals form the subject of not a few anecdotes. The outward smartness of an empty-headed lieutenant is often more valued than an intelligent and studious subaltern. Drink, gambling, and coarse dissipation are of frequent occurrence. The pay is miserable, and poverty-stricken officers are captains at the advanced age of forty-five, while those who have interest are sometimes generals at thirty-five. Probably the author describes his own sad experiences in the *Army* as distinct from the

Guards, which, however, form only about one fiftieth part of the whole Army. An ideal general is the subject of another episode. He finds that real work is more important than endless written reports which are still the order of the day. The good general tries to counteract the evils of routine, but he is maligned at head-quarters.

Mr. Egorov's strictures remind us of a characteristic chestnut anecdote which we heard many years ago about bribery, but we trust that it does not apply to the present times. An official of the Commissariat was sent from St. Petersburg to the South of Russia—a distance of some 2,000 miles—when no railways or telegraphs were extant. He was entrusted with the building of wooden store-houses, the purchase of grain and cattle, which was to be fattened, killed and salted.

The official wrote frequent and regular reports to his authorities about the purchase of timber, grain, cattle, of the hire of pasturage and of the salting of the meat. But his very last report stated that by the will of God the store-houses and all in them had been destroyed by fire.

He had done nothing, had pocketed the money,· but *on paper* he was all right.

The present achievements of the valiant Russian Army disprove the strictures of M. Egorov.

LA RUSSIE INTELLECTUELLE.

Par Louis Leger, Membre de l'Institut, Professeur au College de France (Maisonneuve, 3 rue du Sabot, Paris, 1914).

The author is a specialist in Russian literature, as testified by a long list of works. We remember reading some of his productions in the " Bibliothèque Universelle."

We should explain that *intellectual* does not mean the *intelligenzia* of Russia, that latest excrescence of Slav civilization.

M. Leger has had access to new and original sources of information, unknown to Western readers.

Under his dexterous pen, Russia reveals novel attractions of national lore.

The first part of the book contains a historical account of Russia, amplified by the chronicles of monks and by popular legends. The conversion of Russia to Christianity, the Tartar bondage, the defeat of the Tartars by Dmitry of the Don and the final destruction of their power, turning them into hewers of wood and drawers of water, are picturesquely described.

En 1486 la Horde d'Or cessa d'exister. Ou sait comment Ivan le Terrible, par la conquête de Kazan et d'Astrakhan (1551-1554), assura à la Russie le cours entier du Volga ; comment la seconde moitie du XVIII. siècle, Catherine conquit la Crimée. Maitresse de la Mer Noire et de la Caspienne où débouchent ses grandes fleuves, la Russie pouvait à son tour prendre l'offensive contre l'Asie et pousser ses armées victorieuses jusqu'au littoral de l'Océan Pacifique.

The artificial splendour of Catherine's reign, with its glamour of literature and philosophy, form the subject of the next picture. Derjavin's adulatory poetry and von Vizin's critical plays added lustre to the policy of the Empress and to her desire to pose as an author and a friend of Voltaire and Grimm.

Monsieur Leger introduces several personages who figured in Russia but have not been brought forward like the more hackneyed representatives of Russian literature, whose names have become familiar to our quasi reading public.

"Un homme d'état Russe du Temps passé" is Count Paul Strogonov, a descendant of the great merchants in the Ourals, whose adventurous servant, the rebel Cossack

Ermak, conquered Siberia. One of the Strogonovs was a famous soldier, and an able diplomatist as Russian Ambassador in London.

The historical researches of the Grand Duke Nicolas Mikhailovitch have assisted M. Leger in this study.

" Les Amours d'un Idealiste " is the story of the poet Joukovsky, the translator of Schiller, and the author of some famous sentimental poetry.

" Le Poète National de la Petite Russie " is Taras Schevchenko, the son of a cobbler and the figurehead of the Malo-Russians. After some official opposition a monument is to be erected to his memory at Kiev. His exile to Siberia had endeared him to his own countrymen in the Ukraine.

" Un Poète Russe " is Koltsov, the son of a cattle dealer, whose poetry reminds one of Burns and has an everlasting charm.

" Le Roman d'une étudiante Russe " is based on the " Journal d'une femme Russe," by Elizabeth Diakonov, concerning her existence in Russia and in Paris. It reminds one of Marie Bashkirtzev's well-known Diary, so much admired by Mr. Gladstone. Miss Diakonov is an interesting, typical, superior specimen of a talented but painfully neurotic Slav young lady, who died an early death, worn out by over-wrought excitability but full of noble aspirations and charitable schemes for the good of misguided humanity.

" L'autre Tolstoi " is perhaps as great an author as his relative, the more renowned Count Leo Tolstoy. The former was connected with the highest families of the realm, and was a playmate of the Czar-Liberator Alexander II. Some twenty years ago his great novel, the " Silver Prince," descriptive of the horrors of Ivan the Terrible, was translated into English. Count Alexis Tolstoy (his cousin spelt his own name *Tolstoy* in English) was a prolific author. His poetical productions are varied, beautiful in form, and abounding in wit and kindly criticism.

Last but not least we come to " Alexandre Ostrovsky,'' whose comedies of Moscow merchant life were as popular in Russian theatres as Gogol's exposure of the officials— the *chinovniks*.

We have pointed out the headings of M. Leger's most recent work—the fruit of study, experience and love of Russia. It merits to be widely known, and the up-to-date, masterly French is an additional attraction.

AN ECONOMIC HISTORY OF RUSSIA.

By JAMES MAVOR, Ph.D., Professor of Political Economy in the History of Toronto. Vol. I : The Rise and Fall of Bondage Right ; Vol. II : Industry and Revolution. (London : Dent. New York : Dutton.)

Noticed by F. P. MARCHANT.

THIS important work is far wider than its title indicates, as the industrious author incorporates a vast mass of political and general history and legal discussion into his narrative. He acknowledges indebtedness to the Imperial Ministry of Finance and other State departments, Zemstvo authorities, Columbia University, Professors Sviatlovsky, Kaufman, Odarchenko, Den, and other Russian friends. He also makes considerable use of the history by the late Professor V. Kluchevsky, of which the successive volumes of Mr. Hogarth's translation have been noticed in our *Proceedings*. The above will suffice to show that Dr. Mavor has gone to Russia itself for materials, and to unimpeachable sources.

The first volume starts with the Eastern Slavs of the Carpathians, the trading towns and petty principalities, and the ultimate organised groups.

The conflicts between local autonomy and imperial autocracy which were waged in Europe throughout and after the Middle Ages,

had their counterparts in the struggles between the Russian free towns
and rural principalities on the one side and the Moscow princedom on
the other. In Europe the imperial idea gave way before the idea of
nationality; but in Russia the imperial idea was victorious, town after
town, principality after principality passed under the control of Moscow
and came to be welded into one political whole.

Referring to Peter's reforms, Dr. Mavor finds that the
extension of education among people who did not welcome
it was not always happy. With cadet corps, academies, and
gymnasia, " the products of this artificially forced system
were the ' green young men ' of Griboyedov's comedies."
He finds parallels to this state of affairs among young
Chinamen half educated in America, and in India among
students of Western European culture. A parallel to Russia
under the Empress Anne, when eyes were turned to Europe
in search of a new political system, is found in modern
Japan, which looked to European forms of government for
guidance. The European attitude towards eighteenth-
century Russia, says our author, resembled that of the
Powers towards nineteenth-century China. Peter, alive to
this, said : " Europe is necessary to us for some decades, and
afterwards we will show it our back."

The peasant problem in all its bearings occupies successive chapters. There is the unique position of the *dvorovie
liudi** in the eighteenth century, from among whom came
talented actors and musicians, many of eminence but still
serfs. Compulsory education was resented ; as a natural
consequence there was dissatisfaction with bondage without
chances of improvement. The revolt of Pugatshov is
traced out as a consequence of Peter the Great's reforms.
Peter treated the nobility with the contempt which they
showed to their peasants, and when the nobility were released from obligatory service later the peasants looked for
relief from obligations to their lords. Here is a tribute to

---

*Serf house servants.

the dogged endurance of the Russian peasantry in the account of the Mountain Works* troubles :—

They were vanquished continuously, and yet the survivors continued the struggle. What the peasants of the Mountain Works did in the fifties and sixties of the eighteenth century is simply what the Slav peoples have been doing always. They may only be finally conquered by extermination, and they are too fecund to be exterminated.

The dislike of the peasants for the factory system and its productions forms interesting reading, and the author notes that contempt for shop goods exists among French-Canadian *habitants*. The goods produced at home were durable and often beautiful, while factory goods were associated with waste and immorality.

The first volume closes with valuable appendices on the orography, climatology and hydrography of the country, and an ethnographical sketch of the Russian people, with statistics of the peasant population.

In the introduction to the second volume Dr. Mavor discusses the phenomenon of violence in revolution, due largely to the operation of deadly logic. Indeed, our readers will readily recall examples of sturdy martyrdom not confined to one party or class. " Disregard of consequences has indeed been elevated in Russia to the dignity of a principle of morals." An important factor in revolutions, of which historical instances are given outside Russia, is the youth of revolutionary leaders, *e.g.*, in the French Revolution. Tolstoy's condemnation of all violence, sometimes impossible to avoid, "partly because of the incompatibility of meekness and government," is based upon profound knowledge of Russian traits. Cossacks and peasants, who differed materially in experiences and ways of thought, looked for wonderful pronouncements from the Crown which should confer freedom and wealth in an

---

* *i.e.*, in factories and mines.

instant, and were often victimised by sham edicts and designing upstarts. Besides Pugatshov there were four other personators of Peter III. Following the influence of the French Revolution and the *Dekabristi* episode, many pages are devoted to Marx, Owen, Chartism and the story of social revolt, in which Russia is necessarily lost sight of at times, after which the *v Narod, Narodnaya .Volia* and Social Democratic movements are described.

This comment on England and Russia in the Far East is important :—

The attitude of Russia towards Asiatic peoples and the rule by her of subject races in Asia are less humane. conscientious and educative than the attitude of England and the rule by her of Asiatic subject races ; but the Russians who exercise the administrative functions in the East are naturally more affable than the English. Both, no doubt, have the faults of their qualities ; but the Russians are habitually more indifferent than the English, and when hostile, much more hostile to moral and religious propagandas which disturb the settled course of Asiatic life and affect profoundly the social structure.

In a footnote, Dr. Mavor hints that the fact that the Orthodox Church does not proselytise spares Russia from friction elsewhere, due to missionary effort to influence Asiatic life, the cause of occasional diplomatic difficulties.

We must reluctantly draw to a close. There is a brief but informational chapter on particularism, and the examinations of the present conditions and the factory system are exhaustive. The expression *intelligensia*—said to be due to P. D. Boborikin as *Nihilist* has been traced to I. Turgeniev's " Father and Sons "—is the subject of a comparison of the educated classes in Russia and Western Europe. Useful and condensed biographies of prominent Russians are frequently given in the form of footnotes, *e.g.*, Prince Mestshersky, Bakunin, Stepniak, Herzen and Dostoievsky. Suffice it to say that the serious student has here a rich mine of study, in which his difficulties have been anticipated and elucidated for him.

Professor Mavor's transliteration of Russian names is unfamiliar and not always exact, as in such forms as Golētsin, Mēlutin, Tsherbatov, Metshersky and *Seytch* (Cossack Republic). There are some repetitions, and we read three times about the Little Russian nickname for the Great Russians, " goats." The age of Bielinsky at death is given as " forty-eight," almost in the same place as his years 1810-1848.

A NEST OF HEREDITARY LEGISLATORS.

By IVAN TURGUENIEFF. Translated by Francis M. Davis
(8, Rusthall Park, Tunbridge Wells).

RALSTON and others have translated Turgenev's* " Dvoryanskoe Gnezdo " under various names, and now we hail this old friend under a new title. Generations of Russian gentry pass before us, but none are worthy the name of *legislators.*

When Turgenev, after a long absence in foreign lands, revisited Moscow for the last time, his countrymen gave him a cold reception. His Liberalism and criticism of the futile existence of the *petite noblesse* wounded the vanity of his peers.

A Moscow professor, who tactfully counteracted the painful impression of the reception, repeated to us what Turgenev had once said, that " thoughts assumed the form of pictures in his mind's eye." We may add : Turgenev was so great a linguist that the style of his French works is as splendid as his racy Russian prose.

Mr. Davis, the able translator, has pointed out in his Foreword that:—

When the simplicity and naturalness of the language of Turgenieff

* We adhere to Professor Morfill's plan of shortening the spelling of Russian names.

are reproduced in English translations of his writings, he will become at least as great a favourite with English readers as George Eliot is, to whose art the art of Turgenieff bears a strong resemblance.

On another occasion Mr. Davis wrote :—

The humanising value of international classical literature is not yet generally appreciated as it ought to be.

We may quote an additional fact : the characters in the best Russian novels are more *life-like* than those in most English novels. Those who venture to criticise the great artist, admit his knowledge of the human heart, but they think that Turgenev's literary pictures are rather copies of life models than creations of a powerful imagination! They also aver that his altercation with Tolstoy was not more dignified than the quarrel between Thackeray and Dickens. Literary genius has weaknesses in common with all frail humanity !

The disintegration of the Russian nobility, its incapacity for practical action, its estrangement from real life, the failure of its best ideals, and the advance of democracy are the ground-work of Turgenev's novels, which deal with Russia from the forties to the seventies of the last century.

The beauty of the grand writer's prose, now rendered into popular English, will scarcely ever be surpassed by any other Russian author !

"THE RE-MAKING OF CHINA."

By Adolf S. Waley.   (Constable & Co., Ltd.)

The author's preface informs us that this work is the outcome of close study of the problems which the recent changes in China have brought into prominence.

The European relations with China are an interesting part of the work :—

In 1897, as compensation for the murder of two German

missionaries, Germany demanded and obtained from China the cession of Kiochau.*

The culminating point of the aggression was reached in 1898, when Russia, who three years previously had taken the lead in forcing Japan to restore Port Arthur to China, compelled China to retrocede that port to the Russian Empire. The result of this move on the part of Russia was to force the necessity upon Great Britain to demand the lease of Wei-hai-wei.†

It is not to be wondered at that, seeing his country threatened on all sides, the Emperor Kwanghsu became more and more convinced that, to save it from disruption, it would be expedient for him to adopt Western methods of government and to organise both his army and navy on modern lines.

With reference to the Chinese revolution and Yuan Shih-Kai, the strong man, who became President, we learn many interesting details. The revolutionary leaders thought to weaken the President's position by securing the rejection by the new Parliament of the Russo-Chinese agreement respecting Outer-Mongolia, which had practically placed itself under the protection of Russia. But, contrary to their expectations, the revolutionary move really improved the relations between Yuan Shih-Kai and the Russian Government.

The author favours us with several pertinent observations and suggestions :—

Many people hold the view that the revolution in China, far from promoting her regeneration as a united nation, is likely to result in her being divided into small independent States, thereby lessening her power in the eyes of the world.

The past history of China does not favour this belief. . . .

The Confucian religion has been the guiding star, the greatest spiritual and moral force in the life of the Chinese nation in the past, as it is in the present, and will be in the future.

The doctrine it teaches is that the Chinese nation is one great family, held together by the fervour of patriotism. The spread of Western education is likely to strengthen that patriotism, and will therefore still further uphold the teachings of Confucius.

---

* History repeats itself, and the "mailed fist" has reappeared to disturb Europe.

† When two men rob a stranger, a third man is bound, in self-protection, to follow their example !

The concluding words of "The Re-Making of China" sum up the situation and the prospects of the Celestial Empire in glowing terms:—

Upon Yuan Shih-Kai, if he, as all well-wishers of China must hope, continues to be the arbiter of her destinies, will devolve the task of giving her a constitution which will satisfy the moderate reformers whilst retaining in his own hands the supreme power of government.

He will also in all sincerity constitute himself the Defender of the Confucian Faith, and thereby combine for his country's benefit the advantages of a modern constitution with the precepts of the sages.

We observe that the author, who admires Confucius, does not refer to the probability or possibility of China being converted to Christianity, as suggested by English missionaries, nor to the great rebellion in the time of Li Hung Chang, which was put down by the prowess of our noble Gordon Pasha.

"THE WHITE VAMPIRE."

By A. M. JUDD.   (John Long.)

READERS who revel in mystery, conspiracy and complicated love affairs will appreciate the author's ingenuity in describing the sensational intrigues of a revolutionary lady, who is not unaptly styled "The White Vampire," an imaginary or fabled demon, said to be a person who, after death, returns nightly to suck the blood of the living, as the dictionary has it!

St. Petersburg, where the plots are hatched, is thus described :—

A city of contrasts. Magnificent palaces, mean hovels, stately cathedrals, broad promenades, squalid streets, all go to make its component parts. It is in the small houses and mean streets where most of the treasonable plots are hatched and plans formed that, when put into execution, startle the whole civilized world.

To lend local colour, we are initiated in the details of the Russian cuisine :—

There was salt cod from the distant coast of Archangel ; there was yellow caviar, which is as tough as gutta-percha, very unlike the expensive grey "pearl" caviar of the sturgeon, which only the rich can afford; there was salted meat and sour cream, flanked by some bottles of beer, and that indispensable article in Russian houses, high or low, the "Samovar," or self-boiler, the Russian tea-urn, with the tumblers and spoons, and lemon cut in slices for the due consumption of the favourite beverage.

Some of the intricate incidents of the story refer to treacherous crimes on the lines of Azev, who ran with the fox and hunted with the hounds by pretending to be a revolutionary while acting as a police spy.

Russians and Russian Jews abroad come in for a share of attention, for they are numerous in the Zürich University, and are even founding their own university in Switzerland, where revolutionary ideals are not tabooed.

Bombs and Siberia are not overlooked in order to add dramatic interest to the exciting romance.

Real and imaginary denunciations against the powers that be are eloquent :—

There are girls, young, tenderly nurtured, well-bred as you are, who have joined the ranks of the oppressed, who have undergone incredible hardships in the cause of liberty and freedom, who are striving for the emancipation of the down-trodden and crushed masses who are kept under, robbed, murdered and ruined by men who, with all their pretence of religion, can order their fellow-beings to be starved, flogged and tortured, who can order delicate women to be incarcerated for no other reason than that they dared to raise their voices in the sacred cause of liberty.

WITH POOR IMMIGRANTS TO AMERICA.

By Stephen Graham.　　(Macmillan & Co.)

Mr. Graham has extended his horizon from the Old World to the New.

Everything he has told us about Russia has been true and interesting, showing his sympathy for the people and his love of their country. Now he takes us to the United States and also displays judicious appreciation of American idiosyncrasies.

The prologue opens with a comparison between the two countries :

From Russia to America; from the most backward to the most forward country in the world ; from the place where machinery is merely imported or applied, to the place where it is invented ; from the land of Tolstoy to the land of Edison; from the most mystical to the most material ; from the religion of suffering to the religion of philanthropy. . . Russia is the living East ; America is the living West—as India is the dead East and Britain is the dying West (?) Siberia will no doubt be the West of the future (?)

A remarkable feature of our author's genius is the ingenuity with which he brings out important and instructive national traits of character by means of apparently trivial conversations and passing incidents as he tramps along Russia and America. Here is an example of a Russian immigrant going to the United States :

Alexey was a fine, tall, healthy-looking peasant workman in a black sheepskin. . . You see all I've got is just what I stand up in.

Both he and his friend (a broad faced Gorky-like tramp) took communion before leaving Astrakhan. I asked Alexey whether he thought he was going to break his faith as the other Russians had said to a Jew. How was he going to live without his Czar and his Church ?

He struck his breast and said : "There, that is where my Church is ! However far I go I am no farther from God !" Would he go back to Russia. He would go back to die there.

"Tell me, said he, do they burn dead bodies in America ? I would not like my body to be burned. It was made of earth, and should return to the earth."

In a chapter entitled "American Hospitality," Mr. Graham throws new light on an old subject.

It is possible to distinguish two sorts of hospitality, one which is given to a person because of his introductions, and the other which is given to the person who has no introductions—the one given on the the strength of a man's importance, the other on the strength of the common love of mankind. America is rich in one species, she is not so rich in the other. . . New York seemed to me more friendly and hospitable than any other great city I have lived in. . . .

But when I shed respectability and the cheap fame of having one's portrait and pages of " write-up " in the papers and put pack on back, and sallied forth merely as a man, I found that the other and more precious kind of hospitality was not easily come by. Little is given anonymously in the United States.

There is an amusing chapter on " The American Language " and other interesting subjects, which did not strike Charles Dickens and more recent writers and travellers. The present writer has never crossed the Atlantic, and has learnt and enjoyed much, thanks to Mr. Stephen Graham's graphic pages.

LETTERS OF FYODOR DOSTOEVSKY

To His Family and Friends.

Translated by Ethel Colburn Mayne.

(Chatto & Windus.)

THE frontispiece is an excellent likeness of Dostoevsky, just as we saw him at St. Petersburg on his return from Siberia. Among his letters some are addressed to his brother Michel and Apollon Maikov, whom we also met at the house of our old Russian teacher, A. P. Milukov*. The latter wrote " Recollections of Dostoevsky " as far back as 1848-1849. Always unpractical and in trouble about money matters, the Russian mystical idealist was ever under the influence of noble and humanitarian aspirations, so much in harmony with his genius. His faith in Orthodoxy and in Russian religious sentiments, was unbounded. He even imagined that they would regenerate the whole world.

The newspaper which the brothers Dostoevsky started proved a dead loss. Michel was the better editor of the two,

---

* We write Milukov and not Milyukov as in the text, because the Russian letter Ю is pronounced exactly as our U.

as A. P. Milukov once told us, but with all their talents, they had no idea of business. Debts created enemies, and they had a bad time of it.

Among interesting letters, we must name those which are addressed to literary men like Maikov. We were not, however, aware that Dostoevsky got himself transferred from the military to the civil service through the intercession of General Todleben, the great engineer of Sevastopol fame.

The following inmost thoughts, written by Dostoevsky to Maikov, are very characteristic. He writes from Florence, pursued by creditors and tormented by illness :

These cursed creditors will kill me to a certainty. It was stupid of me to run away to foreign lands ; assuredly 'twere better to have stayed at home and let myself be put in the debtor's prison. . . . Now, here is what I propose :

A long novel entitled " Atheism " ; before I attack it I shall have to read a whole library of atheistic works by Catholic and Orthodox-Greek writers. Even in the most favourable circumstances I can't be ready in two years. I have my principal figure ready in my mind :

A Russian of our class, getting on in years, not particularly cultured, though not uncultured either, and of a certain degree of social importance, loses *quite suddenly*, in ripe years, his belief in God. His whole life long he has been wholly taken up by his work, has never dreamed of escaping from the rut, and up to his forty-fifth year has distinguished himself in no wise. (The working-out will be pure psychology : profound in feeling, human, and thoroughly Russian.) The loss of faith has a colossal effect on him. . . . He tries to attach himself to the younger generation—the atheists, Slavs, Occidentalists, the Russian sectarians and anchorites, the mystics : amongst others he comes across a Polish Jesuit ; thence he descends to the abysses of the Chlysty-Sect* ; and finds at last salvation in Russian soil, the Russian Saviour, and the Russian God. . . .

My dear friend, I have a totally different conception of truth and realism from that of our " realists " and critics. My God! if one could but tell categorically all that we Russians have gone through during the last ten years in the way of spiritual development, all the realists would shriek that it was pure fantasy ! And yet it would be pure realism.

---

*Flagellants.

This excerpt may, perhaps, afford more insight into the heart and mind of the original author than pages of his ordinary letters and writings.

In rendering Dostoevsky into English the translator has probably been assisted by French and German translations, of which mention is made in the Preface.

The present volume derives chiefly from the book by Tchechichin: "Dostoevsky in the Reminiscences of his Contemporaries and in his Letters and Memoranda." (Moscow, 1912.)

We conclude by expressing our gratitude, in the name of all lovers of Russian literature, to Miss Mayne for her excellent translation of a most original author, whose reputation has been growing by leaps and bounds in his native land and whose genius has not yet been sufficiently understood among English-speaking people.

JEWISH LIFE IN MODERN TIMES.

By ISRAEL COHEN.   (Methuen & Co.)

A COMPREHENSIVE description of the Jewish people is, perhaps, a novelty for our public.

As the Preface states, the work presents:—

A General Survey, showing the dispersion and distribution of Jewry in its countless manifestations, its diversity of composition in political and spiritual respects, and the solidarity that unifies its disparate elements.

The extraordinary ability displayed by Jews in Art. Science, and especially in Business, as well as the generosity exercised by some of their merchant princes, are certainly worthy of the admiration and appreciation of all fair-minded and impartial persons.

The author observes that the sufferings of the Jews in Russia and Rumania have been more galling and desperate than those of the Jews in certain Oriental lands. He says:—

The bondage of the Jews in Russia consists in a multitude of laws which rob them of all liberty in the choice of domicile and occupation, which cripple their opportunities of education, limit their right to own property, exclude them from State and municipal service, and impose heavy burdens upon them in regard to military duty. . . . .

The plight of the quarter of a million Jews in Rumania is in several respects even worse than that of their brethren in Russia. . .

The material position of the great majority of Jewry defies description. Only a small portion of those settled in Western countries enjoy the wealth that is commonly attributed to the entire race; but in the regions containing more than two-thirds of the world's Jewry—Eastern Europe, Western Asia, and Northern Africa— there is a depressing spectacle of widespread poverty and misery.

All matters explaining the position and condition of Jews all over the world are worked out with great industry and detail.

In the chapter on "Zionism" we were, however, surprised not to see the name of the late Mr. Edward Cazalet,* of Fairlawne, Kent, for he had been very active in his desire to improve the condition of the Jews by their colonization in Palestine.

In fact, it was only his untimely death, which occurred at Constantinople, whither he had gone to obtain the concession of the Euphrates Valley Railway, some thirty years ago, which arrested the execution of his plan to colonize the Jews in Palestine.

Mr. Cohen's work requires not only to be read, but also studied, for it contains a fund of special information which should be more known by all civilized people.

"THE RUSSIAN ARMY FROM WITHIN."

By Wm. Barnes Steveni. (Hodder & Stoughton.)

Mr. Steveni knows all about the Russians, and his book contains even more general information about Russia than the title conveys.

---

*A cousin and namesake of the President of the A.R.L.S.
See "Palestine and War," page 98.

The author thus introduces his subject :—

It is now a thousand years ago since the Slavonian chieftains of the ancient city of Novgorod sent a deputation to the Varangian Rus on the other side of the Baltic, begging them to come and rule over them, for, said they, *their country was great and vast, but there was no order.*

Mr. Steveni does not share the opinion of many cynical critics that the Russian Army is always more numerous on paper than in reality, for he writes :—

I am inclined to believe that the effective fighting force is even greater than is officially announced.

The Russian Army is recruited principally from the peasant class, and from various nomadic races inhabiting the eastern provinces. . . .

Their physique is very fine as compared with that of other European races. . . .

If the mortality is enormous, however, the birth-rate is astonishing.

When we take into consideration the inexhaustible resources in men, money, and material which are at the disposal of the Russian Government, it is difficult not to believe that Russia will emerge victorious from the terrible racial and political struggle against the combined forces of Austria and Germany, provided that her officers and generals are on a line with her brave and hardy soldiers, and that the alien races subject to her sway remain loyal during the war.

The chapters on " Uniform, Arms, and Artillery," on the " Japanese War and its Lessons," and " The Cossacks " furnish much interesting information of which the British reader is ignorant.

Justice is done to General Kuropatkine, who was handicapped by those who were above him, although it was no secret that his former chief, General Scobolev, reproached him with want of *decision.*

Mr. Steveni spent much time in the company of Russian officers, and relates particulars which could not be obtained otherwise than by personal intercourse.

An evident error is committed by spelling the name of the present Minister of War, General Suchomlinoff— *Suchomiloff !*

The author does not criticize the military schools, which

are, however, not perfect as regards physical development and general health. Out-of-door games, like in our public schools, are not the order of the day.

As regards Russia's offensive power, we must not omit to repeat the author's telling remark : —

> It entirely depends on the internal political state of the country; and on this depends essentially her success in the terrible struggle.

A Russian writer, whose name is not given, says :—

> In truth, the whole world now beholds what terrific proportions modern warfare can attain, and one involuntarily asks the question, What is going to happen next, if we proceed still further—in our Christian era—in perfecting the implements of mutual destruction? There can only be one answer to this question : Humanity is marching towards self-destruction. War will thus become an absurdity, since all the belligerents will become mutual exterminators of one another; and the word " victor " will bear the same meaning for all—Ruin.

"THE FAIR LADIES OF THE WINTER PALACE."

By Dr. A. S. Rappoport,

Author of " Love Affairs of the Vatican."

(Holden & Hardingham.)

THE author appears to have a leaning to the seamy side of history, in which Popes and Tsars, and more or less fascinating representatives of the fair sex, are exposed, with all their human frailties.

Woman's lot in Russia before the iconoclastic Peter the Great and down to the fair mysterious pretender— Princess Tarakanoff, whom Prince Bariatinsky, the husband of the popular actress, very lately described in one of our periodicals— forms the subject of more than 300 pages, and 20 illustrations of the principal personages.

Peter the Great, in his complicated matrimonial arrangements, was quite worthy of our Henry VIII, and his many love-affairs and *liaisons* might hear comparison with the voluptuous proceedings of Louis XIV, *le grand monarque.*

Peter's execution of his Swedish mistress and of his son Alexis is related with ghastly minuteness. Catherine I, Elizabeth I, Peter II, Catherine II, form a sanguinary galaxy in which dramatic love affairs and crimes of every degree are told with details.

The author does not entirely condemn the reforms of Peter the Great concerning women as some Slavophils have done : —

The Tsar gave women the possibility and opportunity to abandon the former life of Byzantine piety and austerity, and to become less faithful to their conjugal duties than they even had been before. But, on the whole, Russian women owed a debt of gratitude to Tsar Peter. . . .

The freedom, therefore, which Peter the Great had granted the women of Russia, although at first instrumental in fostering a laxity of morals, in the course of time helped to develop the energy of the former slave, and enabled her to regain her independence in general life. The influence and power of women soon became paramount. The former slaves began to rule, not only as Tzaritzas, but as frequent advisers of either their husbands or lovers, and Catherine I was not the only woman who exercised a political influence during the eighteenth century.

"SHIFTING SANDS."

By Alice Birkhead.   (John Lane.)

THE accomplished lady-author has not only written novels— "The Master-Knot," etc.—but has made a study of various phases of Russian history. Her lecture on Peter the Great, which was delivered before the Anglo-Russian Literary Society, is printed in our last issue, No. 70, and contains valuable and interesting information. "Shifting Sands" is dedicated "To N.R.H., in Memory of Devon Days."

We think of Charles Kingsley when we read the opening lines of the romance —:

The violence of early spring dashed the Atlantic waves against the coast of Westward Ho! There was the strange shriek caused by the fury of the tide upon the Pebble Ridge, the splendid murmur of the deep cauldrons that lie below the cliffs of Abbotsham.

There is nothing trite or commonplace in the descriptions which flow from Miss Birkhead's pen, nor in the characters created by her imagination. There are subtle and delicate shadows in the delineations of her *dramatis personæ*.

Here is another passage which took our fancy :—

The dirty, picturesque streets of Appledore were crowded with seafaring men, bold girls with comely faces, and happy, red-haired children. An artist stood by the custom-house sketching the quay and the white, distant gleam of Instow. A boat was dawdling across the ferry, rowed by boys with muscles strained, though their exertion did not seem to make much headway. An old sailor with a knowing eye looked approvingly at Gabrielle as she turned the corner of the ship-building yard with the swinging step that revealed her strength and spirit. "A bonny Devon lass," he said to himself, though she had none of the ruddy plumpness that is associated with the country.

We are introduced to the heroes and heroines of the novel when they are children and follow them through life, which increases our interest in their careers. They get restless and want to do something—a very common and natural wish. As the narrative advances we follow the development of various characters as they are moulded by the author.

We will not spoil the pleasure which is in store for intelligent readers by prematurely revealing the plot and details of an ingenious and thoughtful story.

THE RUSSO-JAPANESE WAR, FIRST PERIOD— THE CONCENTRATION.

Special Campaign Series.

By Capt. F. R. Sedgwick, R.F.A.   (Geo. Allen & Co.)

Notice by W. F. Harvey.

In the tenth volume of "Special Campaign Series," Capt. F. R. Sedgwick begins with a masterly summary of the political events that led up to the war with Japan, and points out lucidly that for the latter country the issues were not only political and economical, but also moral. Hitherto, the onward march of the Europeans across the Continent of Asia had met with effete governments and nations whose opposition was easily overcome. The Chinese being a commercial race and the Japanese a race of sailors and warriors, the latter were naturally the fittest of the Mongols to try conclusions with the white aggressors. "There is no doubt," writes Capt. Sedgwick, "as to which of the two great Mongol races stands highest in the estima- tion of the world to-day. . . . That position has been won by the sword, and must be kept by the sword. *Is it not possible that there may be some lesson in this for the British people ? "* The italics are ours, and, in the light of present events, for which we have chiefly our slackness to thank, these words, written six years ago, have a prophetic value. The first operations began in February, 1904, when the Japanese despatched a squadron to Chemulpo and another to Port Arthur. This volume concludes with comments on the strategy of the belligerents up to the end of July, and some notes on the tactics of both sides. In compiling this sketch, the author has availed himself of all published sources of information. Twelve maps enclosed in the pocket will prove of the utmost assistance to students preparing for competitive examinations for the Army; indeed, for such it would be hardly possible to exaggerate the value of this text-book.

"THE RUSSO-TURKISH WAR, 1877."

(SPECIAL CAMPAIGN SERIES.)

By Major F. MAURICE. (London: George Allen & Unwin.)

Notice by W. F. HARVEY.

AT the present moment, when Turkey, acting under strong German pressure, has without provocation entered on hostilities with Russia, "The Russo-Turkish War, 1877," by Major F. Maurice, will be read with renewed interest as much by intelligent students of modern history as, perhaps, by candidates preparing for admission to the Staff College. Apart from its great value as a text book it is by no means dull reading, especially in that portion which deals with what is known as the "Eastern Question." The learned author has availed himself of all generally available sources of information, as is shown by the list of books—German, French and English—given in the preface. Three maps are enclosed in the pocket of the volume, viz., of Turkey in Europe, of the country between the Danube and the Maritza, and, lastly, of Plevna's neighbourhood, respectively. The maps and plans are extremely clear, and all unnecessary detail is omitted. This unpretentious book gives a complete history of the campaign, though the final phases of it after the fall of Plevna are summarised. As a strategical account of the war it has no rival.

"THROUGH SIBERIA."

The Land of the Future.

By Fridtjof Nansen, etc., etc.

Translated by Arthur G. Chater.   (Heinemann.)

Two Poles wrote books on Russia: Tegoborski, the author of " Les Forces Productives de la Russie," said that Russia, as regards natural produce, was the richest country, while Wolowski, a Senator under Napoleon III, wrote on the same subject, asserting that Russia was the poorest country in the world.

The famous explorer, Dr. Nansen, appears to take a favourable view of Siberia's productive powers, and probably hits off the happy mean between the two *Poles*.

We have stated elsewhere that if the Russian Government had admitted English goods free of duty into Siberia *viâ* the Kara Sea route, opened out by Captain Wiggins, a member of the A.R.L.S., a quarter of a century ago, everybody would have been the better for it. The great rivers, the Yenisei and the Obi, would have distributed the goods broadcast over Siberia and brought return cargoes of grain, etc., to Europe.

Practically nobody would have been the worse for the innovation, not even the Moscow manufacturers, whose produce has to be transported thousands of miles to Siberia at exorbitant rates of carriage. We are glad that, in substance, Dr. Nansen agrees with us.

The volume which lies before us is of ponderous dimensions, counting near 500 pages, and is supplied with maps and illustrations which are most interesting and helpful.

The adventures and hardships of the sea-voyage are a reality and a romance.

The Samoyedes, Ostiaks and other native races, which we supposed were dying out under the combined influence of *vodka* and other adjuncts of so-called civilization, are presented under new colours not bereft of redeeming qualities.

Dr. Nansen mentions the Russo-German Professor Middendorff, who said that he could leave kegs and bottles of spirits on the tundra without any protection and conceal-ment, and they were never touched by the Samoyedes—drunkards as they were.

The author makes some touching references to an institution which, we hope, has now been relegated to the past. He describes a prominent exile.

He was a big fellow of over six feet, with a powerful face, a fair moustache, blue eyes capable of being either keen or gentle, either very much on the spot or dreamy and far away; a well-developed, powerful chin and a straight nose. He might have been about thirty. . . .

He had served his time of exile, and had been free for the last three years; but he still lived on here alone, summer and winter. . . .

When he spoke of Russia and of his native place, Kharkov, tears came into his eyes. His wife had died a year or two after he went to Siberia, and he had no children. . . .

He had not seen a newspaper for several years, and such things as the Balkan War were entirely new to him. . . . . .

With reference to the colonization and development of Siberia Dr. Nansen quotes a Russian author, who says that:—

The melancholy history of the country confirms in a certain degree the opinion entertained of Russia by several foreign enquirers—that she understands well enough how to conquer new countries but not how to colonize them. . . . .

Further on Dr. Nansen adds :—

The reason for the slow development of the great and rich territories in Asia is doubtless partly to be sought in the fact that until recently the desirability of encouraging and colonizing them was little under-stood in Russia; indeed, they were even looked upon as rivals which it was undesirable to encourage, but which were rather to be exploited for what they were worth. In addition to this there were many other factors. . . ..

It is remarkable that while Russia had these vast territories lying more or less idle she sent every year great numbers of emigrants across the ocean to America ! . . . .

Siberia has other mineral wealth besides gold. Iron is abundant but imperfectly exploited ; there are also copper, silver, lead, etc., etc. . .

The policy of the present Governor-General in the Ussuri Region is to drive the yellow population, especially the Chinese, out of the whole of the Eastern government, as he foresees danger in an inundation of them.

The chapters on the Amur and Transbaikalia are fraught with interest, but we fear that as reviewers we have already made too many excerpts.

Dr. Nansen's fine book, and Mr. Chater's excellent translation, should not only be read but studied by the man in the street, and also by his betters.

Dr. Nansen thus bids farewell to Siberia : —

I have a feeling of sadness on parting from these great, melancholy forests and this solemn scenery, with its broad, simple lines, free from all petty details. I have come to love it, this boundless land, mighty as the ocean itself, with its infinite plains and mountains, its frozen Arctic coast, its free and desolate tundra, its deep, mysterious taiga, from the Ural to the Pacific, its grass-grown, rolling steppes, its purple, wooded hills, and its scattered patches of human life.

"THROUGH SPAIN."

By DUNCAN DICKINSON. (Methuen.)

THIS book is well calculated to afford one all necessary information, founded on experience, how to travel with pleasure and advantage in Spain.

Starting from Petrograd, the first capital in Europe which has changed its name in imitation of Tokio in Japan, the author travels across the continent to Spain. We envy him, for the site of the Peninsular War is a part of Europe which we have not visited.

Northern and Southern Russia are as flat as the hand.

In the north forests and bogs abound, and in the south, between Odessa and the Sea of Azov, all is level and dreary, with the exception of a picturesque corner of the Crimea.

From the Russian frontier to Berlin the railway runs through monotonous surroundings. Says the author:—

The wild, unkempt appearance of Russian scenery, with its endless forests of birch and pine, and its squalid peasant cabins, is gone, and its place is taken by the trim and tidy German landscape, with neat brick houses, and undulating fields and downs. Trees disappear almost entirely, or, where they exist, serve only to mark the long, straight roads. Later on the trees returned, but the air of neatness and method remained. Personally, I found the Russian landscape more to my taste, but it may have been that long acquaintance, and familiarity with its salient features, endeared it to me.

After crossing Germany and France, the traveller reached the Pyrenees :—

The scenery here closely resembles that of Northern Russia, so numerous are the fir-trees. The trunks of these trees are all scored, and the resin which exudes is caught in little cups. . . .

Near Biarritz, the sea came into sight, looking exquisitely calm and blue in the early morning sun.

Madrid produced a depressing effect on Mr. Dickinson, especially the Escorial.

Its associations with the past, present and future Kings of Spain are in no way calculated to raise the spirits of the sightseer.

The historical monuments which the Moors have left in Spain are a source of great interest.

I could see nothing about Granada to imply either ruin or decay; on the contrary, the main thoroughfares, with their electric trams and up-to-date shops, suggested a certain prosperity. . . .

But the *pièce de résistance* is, of course, the Alhambra.

It probably owes its fame to-day, and perhaps even its preservation, to its chronicler, Washington Irving, and it may be that this is the reason why it is so much better known to transatlantic visitors than to our own countrymen.

Washington Irving and a *Russian* friend, of whom little is told, and who was soon called away, were actually lodged in the Governor's apartment in the Alhambra.

. Our author visited Castille and the arid desert of La Mancha, teeming with memories of Don Quixote. On, returning to Madrid the traveller also saw some of the Basques, fine looking fellows, who bear themselves with dignity, being the *oldest race in the world.*

We must not omit to make honourable mention of the thirty illustrations which give a familiar insight into the life and appearance of Spain, with its beauty and originality.

Bull-fighting, that murderous amusement not worthy of the name of sport, is graphically and minutely described, and saves us the trouble of going to look at it.

The conclusion at which Mr. Dickinson arrives is worthy of a good Englishman, who cannot grow accustomed to bull fights, like some foreign residents in Spain have done.

"For my own part," he says, "as I left the Plaza de Toros, I felt that nothing would persuade me ever to see such a performance again."

The author retains, however, favourable recollections of Spain :—

The memories I carried away with me were only pleasant ones.

"UNDER THE WAR CLOUD."

Sermons by the Rev. T. W. Warsey, M.A. (Skeffington.)

THE author preached nine sermons on the war. He considers that the present is " a war against war," and that we are bound to protect justice and humanity against aggression and barbarous violence.

Mr. John Stanhope Arkwright, D.L., has written a Foreword, in which he says:—

A whole host of writers have deliberately preached the doctrine that Might is Right, and so prepared Germany for a policy which tears up treaties and violates every honourable understanding among nations. . . . Before long Europe will realise plainly that no peace can be concluded which does not take into account condign punishment for such defiance of the laws of God and man. . . .

There must be no faltering in the great task, such as would bring shame on our living or dishonour on our dead.

The preacher's last sermon says :—

Let us remember that the Prince of Peace goes forth in this war to conquer the enemy of peace, and let us take heart as we see the nations one after another flocking to his banner. Their mission is that of *peacemakers*, their work to remove the hindrances and obstacles to universal unity. . . . "He that loseth his life for My sake shall find it."

NOTICES OF PERIODICALS.

COTTON IN EGYPT AND RUSSIA.

WHEN presiding at the Congress of Tropical Agriculture in the Imperial Institute on the 29th of June, Lord Kitchener said :—

The successful development of the cotton industry in Egypt depends on most serious attention being paid to the following points :—

(1) The renewal, by purer strains, of the cotton seed in the country, which is liable to deterioration every seven years ; (2) the regulation and improvement of irrigation and drainage ; (3) the proper cultivation and manuring of the land and the rotation of crops ; and (4) an incessant war that has to be waged against insect pests.

A scientific system of irrigation has been laid out on the land at a cost of £10 an acre,* and it was then handed over to the fellaheen in five-acre plots for cultivation (with benefit to all concerned).

Cotton is now, therefore, being satisfactorily grown on a fair proportion of the area, and it is hoped will bring from £15 to £20 an acre. When we consider that there are about 1,500,000 acres of equally waste salt land in the delta waiting for development by drainage, the value of this experiment can, I think, be appreciated.

When travelling in Southern Russia, where every year (and not only a rainy year) would give a good harvest if there existed some reasonable system of artificial irrigation, we were astonished that nothing was done in this con- nection, either by the State or by individual initiative.

As regards growing cotton in Central Asia, things are even less advanced than in Russia. We therefore quote Lord Kitchener's practical remarks in the hope that his experience may be turned to account in Russia as well as in Egypt.

---

* For Russian Central Asia, say, 200 roubles per *dessiatine.*

"RUSSIE ET BELGIQUE.",

This Belgian periodical follows up, step by step, what is being done, or mostly contemplated, in Russia by official commissions, congresses, etc., to modify and alter legislation in commercial and industrial matters. Experience has shown to older nations that less state interference and red tape is beneficial to trade. In this respect it is desirable that Russia should follow the good example set by Western countries.

Our attention is drawn to a new and more complete edition of the standard work, " Histoire de la Russie depuis les origines jusqu'à nos jours," par Alfred Rambaud, 6ᵉ edition, revue et completée jusqu'à 1913, par Emile Haumont, 6 francs (Hachette & Co., Paris). The latest additions comprise the conflict with Japan, the internal troubles of 1905, the manifest of 1905, the first Duma, political parties, Oriental politics, .etc. These additions are due to the pen of M. Emile Haumont and are written in an impartial spirit.

Another useful book of reference for capitalists and business men is, " Seizième rapport annuel de l'Association pour la défense des détenteurs de fonds publics," published at Antwerp. Price 3½ francs.

It treats of various complicated and difficult questions which have influenced the money market, including the Mexican revolution and the war in the Balkans.

" EVERYMAN."

Dr. Charles Sarolea's " Thoughts on the Russian Language " reproduce Prince Bismarck's idea that the study of Russian might supersede Latin or Greek ! The editor of *Everyman* boldly announces in his paper of 17th July :—.

I confidently prophesy that before the schoolboy of to-day will have attained to mature age the study of Russian will take the place of Greek in the schools of Europe. . . .

We hope if Russian is universally adopted that that rich language will no more be disfigured by the wanton introduction of foreign words as seen in the Russian press of the day. We give a couple of quotations with which we can scarcely agree : —

It is strange that reforming Russian despots like Peter and Catherine the Great, although German princes by origin, should have realised the importance of the Russian language as a great moral and political force, and that they should have encouraged its study at a time when even German rulers like Frederick the Great professed nothing but contempt for their national German tongue.

We quite admit that Peter the Great and Catherine the Great realised the importance of the Russian language. We also know that Catherine was entirely German by origin, but it is news for us that Peter the Great was anything but purely Russian by descent!

We were also rather astonished at what a Russian author told Mr. Sarolea :—

I remember Maxim Gorky telling me once that, in his opinion, there were only three men in the whole history of Russian literature who had perfect control of their instrument, namely : Pushkin, Turgenev, and Chekhov.

And how about Krylov, Ostrovsky, Tolstoy, and even Goncharov, etc.?

"EVERYMAN" (No. 97, Vol. IV).

Mr. Aylmer Maude returns once more to his hero— Leo Tolstoy, whose novel, " War and Peace," "exhibits most truthfully the various phases of a soldier's experience."

Some passages might refer to the wicked, devastating war of the present time. History repeats itself.

On the 12th June, 1812, the armies of Western Europe crossed the frontier and the war began. That is, an event took place contrary to all human reason and all human nature. Millions of men committed against one another so great a mass of crime—fraud, cheating, robbing, forging, plunder, arson and murder—that the annals of all the criminal courts of the world do not muster such a sum of wickedness in whole centuries, though those who committed these deeds did not at the time regard them as crimes.

The commentator tells us that Tolstoy's abhorrence of war became still more intensified as a result of the religious outlook on life he then adopted.

His condemnation of war was, no doubt, carried to an extreme; but there is great virtue in the bold challenge of accepted opinions, and his unmeasured denunciation of war, no less than his wonderfully truthful and unbiased descriptions of war, may help on that readjustment of public feeling and opinion which must come if the world is ever to reach a method of settling its international policies without continually endangering the very existence of civilization itself.

"THE NEW WEEKLY."

THE famous traveller, Mr. Harry de Windt, wrote about "Arctic Siberia" on the 18th of July, says *The New Weekly*.

From Irkutsk he went in a sleigh by the frozen river Lena to Yakutsk—a month of continuous travel " through a howling waste of storm-swept ice and snow."

With the exception of great hospitality received from the Chief of Police and other notabilities of the old wooden houses at Yakutsk, his reminiscences of this journey are of a depressing character.

There was luxury and dissipation, but little culture and reading. There were only twenty political exiles, who were free to move about. The traveller saw a few who had become insane ! He concludes : —

The great crowd which had assembled outside Zuyeff's (the Policemaster's) house regarded us as harmless lunatics rather than as possible pioneers of a great railway which might one day encircle the world. Soon after the lights of Yakutsk had faded on the horizon, and I had bidden farewell to a civilisation which was only regained six months later at a gold-mining town in Alaska—Nome City.

FROM THE RUSSIAN PRESS.

1. CRIME IN RUSSIA.

AT Rilsk, in the Government of Kursk, a band of thieves, consisting of schoolboys, has been discovered. The lads, who belong to the local schools or gymnasia, had carried on their nefarious practices for several months without let or hindrance. In the first instance, they robbed the public library and the physical cabinet of scientific instruments. As their guilt was not discovered, they became bolder. They procured firearms, ammunition, daggers and masks; they stole money out of churches, and robbed a widow named Mme. Orlov, who was alone at home with her fourteen-year-old son. Finally they were all arrested, but we have not heard any more about them.

At Novocherkask in South Russia, an official (zasedatel) called Ivanov was condemned to serve five years in a convict regiment (Arestauskaia rota).

He was found guilty of *sixty* crimes committed during a period of two years in the district of Salsk.

He had levied regular charges of five roubles from every trader. In some cases he forced rich horse-breeders to pay him a thousand roubles.

The patience of the inhabitants being exhausted, they presented a complaint to the Government procurator. Ivanov, however, interviewed the complainants, *one by one*, and even threatened them with death, if they did not take back their complaint.

2. AN ARTIST WITH A NEW IDEA.

MANY Russians lament the early death of Mr. L. L. Tatischev, an artist and a poet, who passed away at St. Petersburg, in the spring of this year.

A soldier by profession, he resigned his commission on account of health.

He loved precious stones, saying they possessed an attractive power for him. He even learned the jeweller's art, and created a special workshop, where artistic perfection was attained. His productions had an individual beauty. The director of the Luxemburg Museum in Paris said: " C'est pour la première fois que je vois une idée dans un bijou."

The deceased was also a poet of no mean talent, although he was seldom seen in print, but some of his poetry was put to music. His last verses, " A Soul," were published by the military newspaper, *The Invalid.* The idea and the form of the poetry was touching and beautiful.

---

3. MONKS FROM MOUNT ATHOS.

IN the Office of the Most Holy Synod, and with the concurrence of the Metropolitan and other dignitaries of the Church, several monks, accused of being recalcitrant in their religious views, were admonished by the Assembly met in Conclave. The monks declared that they believed and would believe as required by the dogmas of the Orthodox Church and the orders of the Most Holy Synod. They were invited to kiss the Cross and the Gospels, and after the Church Service the Metropolitan Macarius blessed them. A protocol was signed, and the monks were drafted into various Russian monasteries.

---

4. FUNERAL OF GENERAL A. P. SCHOGOLEV.

THE Russian Press mentions this event, which took place on the 8th of May at Moscow, and states that :—

The Lieutenant-General was 82 years of age. In 1853-54, during the Crimean War, he showed marvellous bravery. When the combined

Anglo-French Fleet bombarded Odessa, the young lieutenant commanded a battery with four guns—the only defence of Odessa. At the end of the fray only one gun remained intact. Schogolev blew up the rest and removed his men. The same day the Allied Fleet left Odessa.

The young officer was decorated with the St. George's Cross. In Odessa a street bears his name and a monument in the form of St. George's Cross is placed to his memory on the spot of the battery.

From official sources we know that the Allies never intended to bombard Odessa, because it was considered an *unfortified* town. It was a mistake to fire on them.

---

5. MAHOMEDANS IN RUSSIA.

MUSSULMAN members of the Duma were authorised by the Minister of the Interior to hold a special meeting in order to consult about contemplated laws concerning their religion. Thirty persons were present. After exposing the mismanagement of successive administrations of the Caucasus, during the last century, Mr. Djafarov summed up the situation by saying that the spiritual existence of a people is its most intimate life and should not be exposed to the tender mercies of local authorities.

It appears that the Mohammedans at the Congress were a very mixed crew — representing Tartars, Bashkirs, Kalmuks and various tribes of the Caucasus.

Mohammedan women in Russia vied with our professors of eugenics by asking that certificates of health should be provided both for men and women before marriage, and that medical inspections should be available if necessary. If " conjugal conditions " are not complied with, either party should have a right to a divorce.

As regards medical inspection the Congress could not meet the ladies' wishes, for there were *no doctors* available !

6. THE ANTIQUITY OF MOSCOW.

WHEN the question was raised of striking a medal (by the Zabelin Library) to commemorate the foundation of Moscow, the exact date was disputed. On the medal 880 is the year, but in history it is 1147. On the site where St. Saviour's Church at Moscow was erected in recent years, two Arabic coins were discovered, bearing the dates 862 and 866.

Moscow was the connecting link between North and South and a resting-place for merchants. Its very name originates from the old word *mostakva*, *i.e.*, the bridge joining North and South. History points out that according to legend, Oleg founded Moscow in the ninth century, and the legend is gradually being turned into a fact.

---

7. NAVIGATION BETWEEN EUROPE AND SIBERIA.*

A RUSSIAN correspondent writing from Siberia reports that nine vessels, including some steamers, arrived from Newcastle and Tronse in Norway in eight days, via the Kara Sea, to the Bay of Varnek.

These ships, purchased of Hamburg Jews, were laden with various European goods. Meeting with no accidents they worked their way, with the assistance of barges, along the great rivers Obi and Yenisei, which are the arteries connecting the whole of Siberia.

RUSSIA—THE PSYCHOLOGY OF A NATION.

AMONG Oxford Pamphlets we find a reproduction of an article addressed to *The Times* by Paul Vinogradoff, the

* "Through Siberia," by Nansen, is reviewed on another page ; also de Windt's "Arctic Siberia."

Liberal Russian Professor, who protests against German pretensions to consider German culture superior to Russian culture.

His *apologia* of Russia gives a galaxy of his country's philosophers, authors and artists, who surpass the Germans. The cruel and barbarous *modus operandi* of the Teutons is **branded**.

The Slavs must have their chance in the history of the world, and the date of their coming of age will mark a new departure in the growth of civilization.

"THE GOSPEL IN RUSSIA."

THIS is an interesting and beneficent periodical, in which our member, the Rev. R. S. Latimer, and his friend, Pastor Fetler, take an active part. The latter relates a touching story how a man who sold *vodka* became converted and finished by selling Bibles to his customers who had become teetotallers.

Principal A. McCaig, B.A., LL.D., the co-editor of this magazine, writes :—

Russia compares favourably with Prussia, and German "culture" seems little removed from the most repulsive barbarism. May we not hope that through Russia's closer relations with the Western powers of France and Britain she may imbibe more of the spirit of true freedom and take a more advanced place in the line of true civilization. . . . Her chivalrous defence of her weak kinsfolk of Serbia wins admiration. . . . Her generous and politic proclamation concerning Poland commands approval and raises the hope that something of the spirit therein shown may steal into her dealings with the oppressed within her borders. Her stern prohibition of strong drink by her soldiers and her people, by which she has sent a teetotal army into the field and practically abolished crime among her civil population, might well be imitated by other more civilised nations.

OBITUARY.

MAJOR P. A. CHARRIER.

THIS splendid officer, who lectured before the A.R.L.S., was a Member of our Committee, and we greatly lament his untimely end, for he was killed on September 3rd while magnificently leading the Royal Munster Fusiliers. The Munsters were cut off owing to a message failing to reach them. The Germans, with overwhelming numbers, worked round the rear of the British battalion and cut it off completely, their position being a loopholed house.

Although twice wounded, Major Charrier continued the direction of the action till after sunset, six hours of intermittent fighting. He was shot a third time and fell mortally wounded.

In spite of the appalling disaster he retained the entire trust and confidence of all ranks to the last, which is the highest praise attainable by a commanding officer.

We regret that beyond a letter printed in the daily press we have not been able to obtain particulars about his early career, for he was an officer who loved his profession and was an expert in military history and science.

NOTES AND NOTICES.

1—VODKA; 2—SANITATION; and 3—TRADE.

1. During the last twenty years the A.R.L.S. has repeated, in season and out of season, that the *vodka* monopoly was the curse of Russia. It is satisfactory that *teetotalism* is now the order of the day, and that the peasantry sympathise with this wholesome innovation.

2. We again express the earnest hope that *sanitation* and *ventilation* may likewise merit the attention of the powers that be Epidemics, increased by war, cases of cholera and plague are rampant; ignorance and absence of elementary sanitation and ventilation are at the root of the evil.

3. The following letter appeared in the *Morning Post* of 16th October, 1914 :—

ENGLAND AND THE RUSSIAN MARKET.

To the Editor of the *Morning Post.*

Sir,—Letters from Petrograd inform me that the Russians are doing their utmost to substitute German goods by British, and that now is the time for English manufacturers to enter the Russian market. As an instance, I may say, that at a meeting of the Russian Red Cross Society, it was stated that various drugs and surgical instruments have of late years been exclusively obtained from Germany, which also supplies Western Europe. This applies to other industries which British manufacturers have lost or have never captured. Example proves that some valuable medicines may now be prepared from *new* materials coming from South America, &c. English specialists and manufacturers should turn their attention to these matters and strike the iron while it is hot.

Yours, &c.,

ED. A. CAZALET,

President of the Anglo-Russian Literary Society.

Imperial Institute, S.W., Oct. 15.

POLITICAL TESTAMENTS OF PETER THE GREAT AND FREDERICK THE GREAT.

PETER'S legendary will was supposed to forecast the conquest of Western Europe, and it is suspected that Napoleon I. invented the existence of this document to excite the world against Russia. German commentators have suggested that the Czar's policy was specially directed against Germany. The present Kaiser, in a speech at Breslau, mentioned an ancient political testament of the Hohenzollerns, evidently favourable to Poland! Now, it is recorded that Frederick II. wrote a will in 1752, which he entrusted to the care of his friend Prince Charles of Brunswick and relegated to his archive. A second political testament of 1768 was preserved in the archives of Berlin. Presumably both testaments advise war and conquest—hence the Kaiser's reference to them.

PALESTINE AND THE WAR.

GREAT Britain had always protected Turkey, which has now declared war! Why not occupy the Holy Land, for it is a scandal to leave it in Moslem custody? Perhaps Catholic and Orthodox people, who fought about the Holy Sepulchre in the Crimean War, would now not object to have it in Christian hands rather than at the mercy of Turkish cavasses. There is a railway from Jaffa to Jerusalem, which is easily reached.

RUSSIAN IN ENGLAND.

Mr. H. E. WELLS visited Russia and returned with the bright idea that Russian should be taught in England on a par with French and German. We have recommended teachers for the purpose.

CONSTANTINOPLE.

NICHOLAS I. was honestly well disposed to England and desirous to avoid the Crimean War. His idea was to make Constantinople a *free-town* under the protection of the Powers. Lord Salisbury truly said : " we put our money on the wrong horse."

ITEMS FROM THE RUSSIAN PRESS.

(*a*) The Government of Chernigov now rejoices in teetotalism. The money formerly spent on *vodka* in one district was *six times* more than the land taxes. Health and money are now saved.

(*b*) In the province of Kutais, in the Caucasus, there are rich beds of *manganese*, which are the property of a German company.

A Caucasian newspaper estimates that during last year the Austrian and German armies have been supplied with *millions of tons* (*!*) of manganese from the Caucasus for purposes of war.

AN OFFICER'S WARNING.

COLONEL C. P. LYNDEN-BELL, a distinguished linguist, since he is an interpreter in Russian and several other languages, delivered in 1903 a lecture, which was printed, on the coming war. It was prophetic. In 1909 he repeated that we were unprepared for war.

A German told him : " There will be no fight ; *it will be a walk-over for Germany.*" Another German regretted that our *homes were so soon to be broken into.*

Colonel Lynden-Bell's concluding remark was : " It is the courage of the politician and not that of the people which is at fault."

POETRY.

TO THE MEMORY OF LERMONTOV.

From the Russian of ANATOLE KREMLÒV.
Translated by WILLIAM HOLLOWAY.

(2/14 October, 1814—2/15 October, 1914.)

" To the West, to the West would I go
" Where flourish the fields of my ancestors,
" Where in a castle on foggy mountains
" Their unforgotten ashes rest."

(From Lermontov.)

A pall lay heavy o'er the land:
    Great Russia mourned her dead,
Pushkin the loved, whose magic band
    The light of song had shed.
'Twas yesterday he struck the lyre
    That freedom loves so well,
And Russia caught the sacred fire
    And felt the magic spell.
And now 'tis mute, the flame is chilled:
    His night shall know no morn.
His blood a heartless blow hath stilled;
    The heavenly strings are torn.
Then, 'mid the people's stony tears,
    A younger voice was heard.
A rushing torrent in their ears,
    A voice that thrilled and stirred.
" Oh! hearken! now that Pushkin's fire
    " And Pushkin's heart are cold,
" For you I string a newer lyre,
    " A younger world unfold.
" To Pushkin's harp I'll tune my lyre
    " With music from his shrine,
" Till Pushkin's soul and Pushkin's fire
    " Shall wake again in mine."

The chords of passion throbbed and beat,
    They owned the master's art.
His was the true Promethean heat
    That kindles in the heart.
On Lermontov, heav'n's favoured child,
    Here on our narrow shore

The world of youth and passion smiled,
And heaped its golden ore.
The world of fancy, Shakespeare's own,
That tortured Byron knew,
Where sightless Milton mused alone,
There was his kingdom too.
'Twas there he sought and found his soul,
And sat among his peers.
He paid the price, the bitter toll
Of misery and tears.
His were the prophet's glow and heat.
He watched the billows flow,
The waves of evil and deceit,
They left him white as snow.
From time to time if life's poor flask
Grew bitter, he would drain
The cup, nor take the gods to task.
He only moaned in pain.

His anguish pierced us, Like the blest
It taught us how to weep,
Like children on their mother's breast
Ere they are lulled to sleep.
His tears were dry in their stony bed
When he felt pain's cruel brand—
'Twas then he recalled the days long dead,
And the voice of his father's land.
For theirs was a land where men are men,
Not chattels bought and sold,
Where chains ne'er clank, and each Scottish glen
Breeds clansmen free and bold.
Far from the home of his sires he was born*
On a distant and colder strand.
But his soul was heavy, his heart was torn
For the sons of his native land.
That laden soul, its grief and tears
Was a gift from the angels of light.
Those dreams that dwell beyond the spheres
He sought through this earthly night.
But could the music of our earth
Recall the songs of the blest?
Peace flew to the heaven that gave it birth.
His soul could find no rest.

---

* Lermontov's ancestors—the Learmonts—were Scotch, but he was born in Russia.

Short was the purgatory here.
Martyr to grief and pain,
Strong, passionate, it knew no fear
But only proud disdain.
The world of mean and little men
Darkened its virgin light,
And lying breath and rancorous pen
Poisoned with deadly blight.
Black ruin had no fears for him :
Death was an honored guest.
On Transcaucasia's mountain grim
He lies in endless rest.
The mountain felt the mortal stroke,
The torrents burst their bed.
Red lightning flashed, and thunder broke
Above the honored dead.*

Translated by WILLIAM HOLLOWAY, B.A. (Oxon),
author of "The New Dunciad", etc., etc.

THE SISTER OF MERCY.

(Literally translated from the Russian of Anatole Kremlòv
by JOHN POLLEN.)

Along the heavy thorn-strewn way
So good, so pure, so full of love
Thou seem'st, with what a holy ray
By halo crowned, to move!

Amidst the sufferings and the woes,
Mid pains of body, pangs of mind,
Relieving these and soothing those,
How sweet thy care—caress how kind !

* 1.—Lermontov died on the 15/27 of July, 1841. His death was announced from Piatigorsk (a spa in the Caucasus) in the following terms :—" On the 15th of July, at 6 p.m., there was an awful storm, with lightning and thunder ; at the same time, between the mountains of Mashuk and Beshtan, Lermontov breathed his last at Piatigorsk, where he was undergoing a cure."

2.—The poetry by A. Kremlòv, "To the Memory of Lermontov," is written in the same metre as Lermontov's verses. At the end of the second part the author adapts some of his lines to Lermontov's "Angel."—"Through the midnight heavens an angel flew."

N.B.—Lermontov was killed in a duel by an officer called Martinov, whom he had ridiculed. We knew the niece of Martinov.

The land War plunges into blood,
The people perish in the war—
Through thy deep love, so pure, so good,
Their sufferings sore assuagèd are!

With one sweet look, one gentle word,
Thou can'st their pain at once suppress,
To hopeless torture balm accord,
To suffering martyrs bring redress!

Thy gentle glance of sympathy,
Of love, alarm, and tender care,
How much it gives of ecstacy!
How loss of strength it doth repair!

Believe me, when thy hours are sad,
All those to whom thy glance gave life,
Whom thy sweet words have made so glad,
With burning love for thee are rife.

They bring thee grateful thanks and high
For all the gifts thou did'st bestow.
Their prayers with pleadings fill the sky
For happy days and peace below.

All blessèd is this life of thine,
And in the name of Right and Good—
Holy to every thought of mine
Sister, of Mercy's Sisterhood!

J. Pollen.

Literally translated from the Russian of Anatole Kremlòv
by John Pollen.

⁂   ⁂   ✳

Stifling! The scorching air
Breathes only fire and gleam.
Tired Nature doth appear
Bewitched, as in a dream.

Exhausted all things stand
Of joy, of hope bereft—
All wait while o'er the land
The thunder-clouds are reft. . . .

Down pours the gracious rain ;
The air grows cool and gay ;
Throughout vast Nature—pain
Floats. like a dream, away.

Ah ! could our people's griefs
By such rain-bursts be stayed,
And drowned in stormy gulfs
Of nation's tears be laid.

J. POLLEN.

SISTER.

(From the Russian by JOHN POLLEN.)

Unknown—a Stranger drawing near—
Beside the soldier's stretcher now—
To all so near, to all so dear—
Sister of Mercy, standest thou.
It may be, thou'rt of noble birth,
It may be, of a class unknown—
To wounded soldier, in his dearth,
Thou com'st like sister of his own.
Where from the foeman's fierce attack
The blood is bursting forth in flood,
Where iron balls the bosom rack,
With cross uplifted, hast thou stood.
A ray of light—with cheering sounds
To soothe the pain hast thou essayed ;
And gentle hands on ghastly wounds
With woman's tenderness were laid.
It was distress that gave you birth
Amongst the rich, amongst the poor,
Ye Daughters of our native earth,
Ye are our sisters, true and pure !
These wounds of ours are wounds of yours ;
This blood that flows—your very own ;
For you, for us, the deed endures ;
To us, to all, one love is shown.
Our Mother Russia from the foe.
Our cruel neighbour, we'll set free !
And Russia's victory all shall know
By steel, and Cross of Calvary.
Unknown—a stranger drawing near—
Beside the soldier's stretcher now,
To all so near—to all so dear—
Sister of Mercy, standest thou !

J. POLLEN.

FROM THE PERSIAN OF OMAR KHAYYÁM.

(Quatrains translated line for line from the original Persian.)

In heart—desire for maiden dear—
In hand—the wine cup all the year;
Men say, "May God to you shrift grant!"
Avaunt! of such I feel no want!

In Inns there's one Lustration—Wine!
A tarnished name no more can shine;
So torn our temperance-veil is here
It can't be mended! So! good cheer!

I saw a man on Palace roof
Who trampled clay without behoof;
The Clay in mystic accents said—
"Cease! You'll be trampled when you're dead!"

Sweet day—wind neither hot nor cold—
Down rose's cheek the rain hath rolled;
The nightingale to yellow rose
Cries, "Wine! drink wine till time shall close!"

Ere Fate attacks thy drooping brow
Let rosy wine be ordered now;
No gold art thou that—witless swain—
Men bury and bring forth again!

Friends! stay me with the wine-cup! do!
To amber face give ruby hue;
Wash me in wine, and when I die,
Let me in vine-planked coffin lie.

King! Heaven decreed thy kingdom's course,
And saddled for thee Empire's horse;
And when thy Charger golden-shod
Touched dust—gilded become the sod.

No worth has Love that's insincere—
No warmth give dying embers here;
No peace—no food—no sleep—no cheer,
Knows Lover true, day, month, or year!

"Forever's" secrets none hath solved;
Nor from his orbit fixed revolved;
Tyro and Teacher, all can see,
Alike in impotence agree.

J. POLLEN.

NOTE.—The quatrains of Omar Khayyám are like sonnets, complete in themselves. They have no connection one with the other, although they are mainly concerned with praise of Love and Wine—or, as the Suhs pretend, with Devotion to the Deity and celestial enjoyments.—J.P.

FUTURE LECTURES.

Paper to be read on the first Tuesday of the following month, at three (3) p.m. :—

1915.

February 2nd.—" ADAM MICKIEWICZ " (the National Poet of Poland), by Miss M. ASHURST-BIGGS, translator of his works.

———

March 2nd.—" REMINISCENCES OF THE RUSSIAN ARMY AND ITS GENERALS," by W. BARNES STEVENI, author of many works on Russia.

———

April 6th.—Mr. ARNOLD WHITE will lecture if possible.

———

No Meetings in January, August and September.

These Lectures are also announced in the leading daily papers.

Patron :

HER ROYAL AND IMPERIAL HIGHNESS THE DUCHESS OF SAXE-COBURG-GOTHA AND EDINBURGH.

LIST OF MEMBERS.

(Up to the 31st December, 1914.)

NOTE.—The numbers correspond to those on Members' cards.
(H.M.) means *Honorary Member.*
(L.M.) means *Life Member,* who has compounded, *i.e.*, paid £10 once for all.

HIS IMPERIAL HIGHNESS THE GRAND DUKE PAUL.

HIS IMPERIAL HIGHNESS THE GRAND DUKE MICHAEL.

637 Abercorn, Duke of	671 Bill, J. H. H., I.C S. (L.M.)
194 Abrikossoff, N. A.	217 Bingham, Capt. W. H.
360 Adams, F. E., R.N.	512 Binsteed, G. C.
645 Adye, Lt.-Col. D. R.	164 Birkbeck, W. J. (L.M.)
475 Alford, A. C.	525 Blackwood, Capt. A. P.
565 Anderson, A. C.	507 Blessig, J. P.
328 Antonini, M.	549 Bobrinsky, Countess B.
325 Armstrong, Major., R E. (L.M.)	345 Bobrinsky, Count V. A.
114 Arsenieff, Admiral	294 Bode, Baron
255 Aschkenasy, S. E.	568 Bode, Baroness Elise
528 Ashby, H. D.	478 Bohac, C.
350 Atherton, Mrs. G. F.	710 Boileau, Major E. A. P.
	523 Bolton, Mrs. A. W.
474 Baer, I.	698 Bonar, Henry, Consul
331 Baldwin, Miss M.	588 Bone, Capt. A. F.
490 Ballard, Lt.-Col. C.R.	662 Boome, Lt.-Col. E. H.
659 Barnes, Major E. (L M.)	627 Borozdin, A. K.
514 Beaumont, S. J.	558 Bosanquet, V. H. C.
35 Beck, Miss (L.M)	238 Boutenoff, Count Chreptovitch
535 Beer, Mrs. (L.M.)	366 Brennan, Hugh
583 Bennett, F. C.	89 Bridge, Major W. Cyprian
545 Bennett, Capt J. H.	404 Britten, Lt.-Col. T. H.
461 Benson, J.	451 Browne, Capt. B. S.
499 Biddulph, General Sir Robert (H M.)	560 Browning, Capt. E. R. L.
286 Bigg-Wither, Rev. R. F.	589 Bruce, Miss A.
466 Bilibine, J.	654 Buchanan, Sir George W.

593	Halpert, R., R.N.
599	Hammond, J. Hays
174	Hanks, Capt., R.A.
482	Harris, E. Legh
312	Harris, Capt. H. T. H.
302	Hartley, H.
270	Hartley, W.
251	Haslam, Capt. B. J.
731	Hastie, Miss J. A. (L.M.)
307	Hausch, A. (L.M.)
108	Havelock, H., M.A.
146	Hay, Major A.
192	Heath, R. L. G.
241	Henderson, Major E. G.
261	Henderson, Dr. G.
371	Henderson-Scott, A. M.
505	Hill, Miss F. Davenport
450	Hilliard, R. (L.M.)
225	Hirsh, H. A.
533	Hobden, H.
460	Hobhouse, Miss E.
158	Holloway, W.
8	Homiakoff, N.
488	Hope, Miss G.
537	Hudson, Major A. R. Ross
233	Ilovaiski, Mrs.
5	Ilyin, General A. A.
580	Johnstone, Miss C. L.
421	Jones, Teague
518	Kell, Capt. V.
666	Kemball, Lieut.-Col. C. A.
418	Kennard, Dr. H. P.
497	Kenny, Capt. W. G. S.
510	Kenrick, C. C.
713	Kingston, Major T. A.
470	Kirby, Mrs. J.
687	Klingenberg, R.
315	Knox, Major A.
512	Koebel, Capt. F. E.

228	Koni, Senator A. F.
214	Koulakovsky, Professor
179	Kovalevsky, V. I.
102	Kremlòv, A.
135	Kühl, C. (L.M.)
342	Kuliabko, Professor A.
489	Lane-Poole, Capt. H., R.M.A.
506	Lane-Poole, Stanley, M.A., Litt. D.
472	Langhorne, Rev. W. H.
442	Latimer, Rev. R. S.
494	Lawton, Lancelot
122	Leger. Professor L.
524	Lepkowsky, J. de
321	Leslie, Lieut. W.
454	Lewellyn-Jones, F.
642	Lewis, Colonel D. S.
686	Lindsay, Lt.-Col. A. B.
143	Lomas, J.
501	London, Bishop of (H.M.)
481	Long, R. C.
248	Lowry, Colonel W. H.
153	Lützow, Count
367	Lynden-Bell, Col. C. P.
675	Lyne, Major C. V. N.
697	Lyons, Capt. G.
273	Macaulay, Major Denzil
282	Makovsky, S. K.
543	Maly, Dr.
492	Masterman, E. A., R.N.
389	Macdonald, Col. F. W. P.
96	Machin, Miss M.
577	McLaren, Mrs.
714	McNeile, Major D. H.
428	Macready, W.
551	Maguire, T. Miller, LL.D.
242	Mappin, Major G. F.
92	Marchant, F. P.
658	Marsh, Major F. G. (L.M.)
587	Massey, W. H. (L.M.)
717	Meakin, Miss A. (L.M.)

393	Mears, A., Major I.S.C.
202	Meiklejohn, K.
185	Milbank, Lady
22	Mirrielees, A. (M.)
74	Morgan, C.
565	Morgan, Capt. M. H. L.
329	Muir, Mrs.
332	Muir, A. H.
598	Murray, Capt. Erskine, R.A.
440	Narischkine, B. G.
453	Neilson, Captain T. F.
355	Newberry Library of Chicago
250	Newcombe, Capt. G. H.
468	New English Club.
618	Newman, Miss C.
372	New York Public Library
394	Nicholas, Ex-Russian Arch-bishop (H.M.)
110	Nightingale, Major M. R.
582	Noyes, Prof. G. R.
439	O'Dwyer, Sir M. F.
161	O'Leary, Col. W. E.
98	Osten-Sacken, Baron Fred (L.M.)
247	Ostroúkhoff, I. S. (M.)
430	Otter-Barry, Capt.
326	Owen, S.
381	Owsiankin, A. W.
365	Parish, Miss M. J.
405	Patrick, R. M. F.
471	Paul, Colonel, R.E
526	Paul, E. M., Consul
31	Perowne, Lt.-Col. J. Woolrych
426	Perry-Ayscough, H. G. C.
47	Peterson, Col. F. H.
562	Phayre, R. B.
581	Phelps, Prof. W. L.
349	Phibbs, Miss H.
23	Philip, W.
613	Phillips, Sir Lionel, Bt.(L.M.)
509	Phipson, M. H.

473	Playne, Miss C. E.
462	Pogson, F. Vere
52	Pollen, Dr. John
39	Poole, Major F. G., D.Ṡ.O.
18	Poutiatine, Countess
350	Prague English Club
207	Prendergast, Col. (L.M.)
348	Preston, E. D. (L.M.)
448	Purcell, Miss
409	Pyper, W. J. Stanton
323	Raffi, A.
561	Ragovin, V.
595	Rason, Capt., R.N.
343	Raymond, Major H. E.
476	Redl, Major
359	Regnart, Capt. C. H.
407	Reinhold, Capt. H. E.
420	Rendall, H. E., R.N.
631	Reval Russian Literary Circle
546	Richardson, Lt.-Col. C.
445	Richmond, R. S.
62	Riddle, J. W., ex Ambassador
368	Riga Russian Literary Circle
311	Ritchie, Rev. A.
579	Ritchie, A. J.
412	Robinson, Miss
151	Robson, Lt.-Col. C. G.
559	Roerich, N. C.
306	Root, N.
571	Rostovtsof, Count I. N. (L.M.)
552	Rowlandson, Capt. H. W.
316	Rowlandson, Capt. M. G.
621	Ruffmann, D. A. (L.M.)
400	Ryle, Miss M. C.
362	Sausey, Count N. E.
594	Saunders, Capt. M.
553	Schéviakoff, Professor V. T.
495	Schishmareff, Capt.
459	Scott, A. Maccallum, M.P.

322	Searight, Lieut. K.	304	Trabotti, A.
159	Sevier, Dr. A.	305	Trabotti, Mrs.
377	Shepherd, Miss G.	384	Trautmann, Miss
720	Shetaloff, Dr. N. I.	354	Travers, Miss R.
608	Shishkoff, N. A.	352	Trevor, Roy
425	Shlehover, A. C.	4	Trotter-Cranstoun, J. Y.
218	Simpson, A. F.	59	Tyrrell, Lieut.-General F. H
385	Simpson, Miss T.	87	Tyszkiewicz, Countess A.
422	Simpson, W. E. D.	597	Van der Vliet, Mrs.
397	Sinclair, W.	603	Van der Vliet, W.
269	Siricius, E., Consul	715	Van Someren, Capt. W. W.,
453	Skaife, Capt. E. O.		D.S.O.
231	Smith, Capt. Rowland	706	Venning, Miss
678	Snowdon, I.	596	Voiékoff, Prof. A. J.
301	Souter, Major A. B.	644	Vostrotin, S. V.
435	Spiers, Miss F.	449	Waley, A.
54	Stebbing, Rev. Thomas R. R.	259	Walker, Major F. H.
415	Steel, H. C.	65	Wallace, Sir Donald
15	Stern, W. (L.M.)		Mackenzie
741	Steveni, W. Barnes	281	Wallis, H. J.
406	Strogonoff, Count	298	Wardell, Major W. (L.M.)
556	Studsen, Capt. A. Ross	340	Wardrop, O.
232	Swayne, Colonel H., R.F	206	Waterhouse, Capt. Claude
60	Sykes, Arthur A.	317	Watson, Major L. A. (L.M.)
180	Talbot, S. C.	477	Watson, Capt. H. D.
458	Taylor, Miss T. M.	536	Watts, E. Ponsonby
12	Tchihatcheff, Admiral	364	While, Miss M.
139	Tchihatcheff, D. N. (V.)	575	White, The Hon. Andrew D.
657	Tennant, Major E.	386	White, Arnold
355	Thesiger, The Hon. W., Consul	491	Whitten, Capt J. E.
480	Thompson, H.	227	Williamson, Dr. G.
173	Thomson, Mrs. H.	432	Wilson, Mrs. E.
61	Thornton, Mrs. (L.M.)	427	Wilson, L. S. (L.M.)
64	Thornton, Capt. W. (L.M.)	80	Wolley, Clive Phillipps
29	Timiriazeff, Professor C. (H.M)	591	Wolseley, Sir Capel, Bt.
78	Timiriazeff, V. I.	274	Woodhouse, A. W., Consul
137	Tollemache, Hon. Mrs. L. (L.M.)	413	Wright, Capt. C. E. Sykes, R.M.
44	Tolstoy, Count M. M.	211	Yaroslav 117th Inf. Regt.
167	Tornauw, Baroness	72	Yeames, W. F., R.A. (L.M.)
369	Tornauw, Baron N.	517	York, Archbishop of
		336	Younghusband, Sir Frank
		341	Zypaloff, A. de

FINANCIAL STATEMENT OF THE A.R.L.S. FOR 1914.

RECEIVED.	£	s.	d.
Balance from 1913	432	7	3
Subscriptions received :—			
For London	24	3	0
„ County and Abroad	56	14	0
„ Life-Members: The Hon. Mrs. Lionel Tollemache, and Mr. E. D. Preston ...	20	0	0
Interest to 31st December, 1914 ...	10	7	6
	£543	11	9
Balance to 1915...	£417	14	11

SPENT.				£	s.	d.
Teas at Meetings				6	18	6
Books, Papers, and Library... ...				9	16	10
"Proceedings," &c., printed ...				62	14	0
„ Stamped and forwarded ...				13	11	9
Imperial Institute				14	12	11
Correspondence, Stationery, &c. ...				18	2	10
Balance in G. P. O. Savings Bank	£415	6	7			
Cash	2	8	4			
				417	14	11
				£543	11	9

Ed. A. CAZALET.
W. H. LANGHORNE.
J. POLLEN.
FRANCIS P. MARCHANT.

Examined and found correct,
CYRIL C. C. KENRICK, M.A. Oxon,
R. S. LATIMER.

CPSIA information can be obtained
at www.ICGtesting.com
Printed in the USA
BVHW081605280119

538839BV00027B/2058/P